That's Why You're Here

Contents

Preface v

Prologue vii

Chapter 1: A Tiny Spark 11

Chapter 2: The First of Many 27

Chapter 3: It's All in the Cards 43

Chapter 4: Taking The Plunge 61

Chapter 5: The Serenity Prayer 81

Chapter 6: Betty's Reading...........................95

Chapter 7: The First Destiny Point 107

Chapter 8: The Teen Years...........................123

Chapter 9: Carson City 141

Chapter 10: Another One 153

Chapter 11: Meeting Dänna 163

Chapter 12: Mom's Passing 179

Chapter 13: A Bit Out of the Norm 195

Chapter 14: A Theme Runs Through It.............209

Chapter 15: My Own Lesson of Free Will 219

Chapter 16: A Work In Progress 231

Glossary 235

Acknowledgments.....................................239

My First Tarot Reading Event....................243

About The Author 244

Preface

$\mathcal{I}$ am often asked by customers, "How did you get into reading the tarot?" This book, in part, details that journey. It also covers my own life stories I was compelled to discuss during many a client's reading. They seemed to find some benefit in hearing my story. We both did. I hope you, the reader of this book, may be similarly touched.

The encounters within are real, but to protect the privacy of clients, family, and friends, some of the names, descriptions, and locations have been changed. True names of people and businesses have been used with permission. The content of my experiences, the readings, and the conversations have been recalled as close to the real events as humanly possible.

Reliving portions of my life has been gut-wrenching and humbling. The lessons learned significant. In the telling of my story, I have searched my soul, and, as some would say, have endeavored to leave all my cards on the table.

Prologue

He sat in his car, hugged by darkness, listening to the rhythmic sounds of the waves.

It was time.

He unscrewed the lid of the pill bottle and dumped several sedatives into his palm. He popped the pills into his mouth, and chased them with gulps of Absolut Vodka. His throat burned. He repeated the ritual until the pills and vodka were gone.

He tossed the empty bottles onto the floor. He patted the envelopes resting next to him.

His wallet and car keys were shoved under the front seat. He got out of the car and quietly closed the door. He would have to move quickly, before the pills and vodka kicked in.

He lifted the kayak that had been resting against the side of his car and made his way to the tiny beach. It was deserted. He unzipped the back of his wetsuit and worked himself out of it, feeling the chilled night air against his skin. His naked body gleamed white in the moonlight. He would go out the way he had come in.

His arms and legs were beginning to feel heavy; his mind was fuzzy. When he stepped into the frigid water it gave his body a jolt. He climbed into the kayak and with uneven strokes paddled through the waves into the bay.

When he was out far enough, he stopped, drained. The ocean held the peace he'd sought, and he was ready to embrace it. He drew his legs up and crouched onto the seat. He raised himself and slipped over the side of the kayak. The cold hit him like a slap in the face. He pushed the kayak away and watched it disappear into the darkness. He could hear the far off roar of waves breaking on the shore.

Suddenly he was wracked by violent shivers. He felt exhausted and numb. He felt bodiless. The tremors subsided and he felt unseen tentacles pulling him down. He struggled to keep his head above the water, but he was growing heavier and heavier. He was so weary from the constant battle to breathe, to live. He needed to rest—just for a moment . . .

1

A Tiny Spark

ecoming a widow plunged me into a grief I was ill-prepared for, and no elixir could alleviate the devastating loss of my lover and friend. The ache in my heart was constant, agony came with every beat, and lingered in the spaces between. I yearned for some insight that might make sense of my husband's death. I had to do something, anything, to fill the emptiness.

I can't remember how it happened. The psychic and spiritual worlds reached out with long sinewy fingers, grasping at me. It could have happened while in a bookstore, the Self Help section I always sought was not far from the Spiritual and Psychic sections. Running my thumb across the spines of several books, I stumbled upon a title that stopped me, *Talking to Heaven*, written by James Van Praagh, a psychic medium. I knew a psychic could tell of future happenings, but I was not familiar with what a psychic medium could do. Quickly leafing through the book, I learned they had the ability to communicate with loved ones who had passed. I purchased *Talking to Heaven*, and raced home. Like a starving person finally presented with a feast, it became the first of many books I would ravenously consume.

The information on the metaphysical, the psychic, and the divine, all resonated deep within me. I liked the idea that there was more to life than what our five senses perceived. I found much of the subject matter fascinating, and was given a measure of peace, thinking our deceased family and friends could be near. This new knowledge led me further into unknown territories, and it felt right.

I wanted desperately to communicate with my husband again, experience some kind of connection, even if it meant going through a third party. Over time, the literature led me to believe that speaking to Kent might be a definite possibility. My dilemma was how to find a medium who was the "real deal." I wanted a recommendation, but no one I knew spoke of spirits or psychic mediums. The subject was taboo. Even so, the urge to contact my husband, though he'd been dead six years, nagged at me day and night. I prayed for help.

The answer to my prayers came by way of Kent's daughter, my stepdaughter, Alice. She had come for a visit. I had known her since she was nine years old, and now Alice was a tall beautiful young woman with long flowing golden-brown hair. She bubbled with energy and brightened any room she entered.

We were sitting at the kitchen table chatting and getting caught up with the latest happenings in our lives, when Alice raised a hand and slapped her thigh. "Oh, I forgot to tell you my aunt did something very unexpected. She got a reading from a psychic medium."

I was stunned. Alice raved about the accuracy of the information that had come through during her aunt's reading. I sensed that this was the medium I'd sought and prayed for. I confessed to my stepdaughter that wanting to communicate with her father had been a secret obsession for years. She understood my desire, and provided me with the medium's contact information.

On the day of the reading, a song stuck in my head, and the lyrics kept repeating over and over, *What a long, strange trip it's been.* I wondered for a moment, *Who sings that song?* Oh, of course, how perfect, the Grateful Dead.

I headed into the Sierra foothills, just east of Sacramento in my electric-blue Nissan Rogue. My hands slipped on the steering wheel from the nervous sweat on my palms. Many emotions traveled through me, but eagerness sprang to the forefront to take the next step in this interesting journey.

Within an hour, I would be meeting a stranger who claimed she could bridge the gap between the spirit world and the physical world. A person who could deliver messages from the dead. Was my desire to connect to my husband clouding my judgment? Was I being foolish?

Was I sure I was ready to do this?

I'd read enough about psychic mediums to know the experience wouldn't be like it was portrayed in old Hollywood movies. There would be no dimly lit room with a crystal ball on a table in front of a wrinkled woman wearing a turban, mumbling in heavily accented English. But what would it be? I didn't know. I did know that learning something from a book, and experiencing it firsthand were two different things. I prayed I wouldn't be disappointed; I didn't know if my heart could handle that.

My destination was the small mountain community of Kyburz. The GPS guided me down a narrow lane of tiny cabins sprinkled among pines. When I finally spotted the address I had been searching for, I pulled into a parking spot bordered by logs, just big enough for my car.

As I stepped from the car, the stillness of the mountain air surrounded me. The quiet was broken as I crunched my way through pine needles to the front door. I knocked nervously. A woman opened the door. She was in her early 60s with long, wavy yellow hair that looked hard to manage, like it needed to be captured and wrangled into a rubber band. She was dressed in sweat pants and sweat shirt. "Hi, I'm Caroline." She smiled reassuringly, and invited me in.

The cabin was chilly and quite small, but otherwise normal looking. Nothing spooky here, just your average cabin in the woods. Caroline motioned me to sit on a moss green love seat while she took the lone wood chair across from me. She said, "I'll be recording the session. Are you ready to begin?"

"I think so," I said, hoping to sound more confident than I felt.

Caroline told me she couldn't guarantee contact with a specific loved one. "It's about the spirits who do show up. Spirits vibrate at a very high and fast frequency, we humans vibrate at a very low and slow frequency. In order for us to connect, I must raise my vibration and spirit must slow theirs down so we can meet in the middle. That's why it's called mediumship."

She closed her eyes, and inhaled and exhaled deeply several times and murmured a prayer of guidance and protection. Her eyes slowly opened, and she stared off into the distance over my right shoulder. I wondered what held her attention. After a few moments, she turned her gaze toward me and we locked eyes. She began, "I have a mother-in-law coming through."

Startled, I thought, *My mother-in-law didn't even like me, why would she be here?*

The medium went on, "She wants to apologize for the way she treated you in the physical. She knows she was not always kind. She has a better perspective now, and is very sorry. Your mother-in-law is also saying you are not with her boy any longer. Is this true?"

"Yes, it's true." Feeling uneasy, *maybe I'm not as ready for this as I thought.* I looked towards the door wondering how I could manage a quick escape.

"Your mother-in-law doesn't want to take up a lot of your time. She knew you were coming today. Spirit passes information amongst themselves when they know a loved one is coming for a reading, so someone you never expected could come through during your time with me." Caroline paused. "Your mother-in-law just wanted to pass on her apology. It's a way of helping her soul's evolution. She says another spirit is helping her to communicate today. Do you know," she tilted her head as if listening, "a David?"

"No, I can't think of who that might be, but please tell her I appreciate the apology." (I later learned David was a family friend.)

"She can hear you," Caroline said. "She's glad you were willing to receive her message. I have another mother energy stepping forward, this feels like your mother's mother. Has she passed?"

I nodded. My grandmother had been a second mother to me, and I'd lived with her for a time as a child.

"She's showing me what she loved, she's baking. It feels like she may send you smells from time to time of something baking when your oven has not been on. She also likes to spend time with you and may ride along in your car. She has a very playful side, so she may adjust things or move items to try and get your attention."

"Well, that is interesting," I said. "I've been noticing that my rearview and side mirrors keep getting moved out of position. I'm constantly having to readjust them and I'm the only person who drives that car. I thought I was losing my mind, but now I know who's behind the shenanigans."

"Spirit can be very playful. If you acknowledge you grandmother, she'll stop with the mirrors."

Shifting in her chair, Caroline said, "Do you have a Tiffany lamp?"

Puzzled by the question, I responded, "Yes, I do."

"Your grandmother is showing me the lamp. She visits you and enjoys this piece. She loved fine furniture, but may not have had much of it herself. She loved very nice things."

My grandmother had been gone for over 40 years. To hear she knew of my lamp was intriguing and touching.

Caroline said, "I'm not sending your grandmother away, but is there someone you'd like to speak to?"

"Kent," I said carefully, not wanting to betray my heart's desire.

Caroline looked away and took a few more deep breaths. Her head whipped back toward me. "Were you married to Kent?"

"Yes," *How did she know that?*

She smiled. "Oh good, because he's showing me a ring on his finger." She stopped for a second. "I just felt an ocean breeze come across my face. Did he like to be on water? Did he own a boat of some kind?"

My head bounced up and down like a bobble-head doll. *This is so bizarre.*

"He's showing me an image, he's on a boat, like a pontoon boat. He's enjoying a lazy afternoon drifting on a river. Kent loves being on water and it's where he was happiest. He's created his own bit of heaven," she explained. Caroline said she believed that heaven was not a "one size fits all" place, each spirit could create their own paradise.

A somber look washed across her face. "Your husband is telling me he's sorry . . . sorry for leaving you so suddenly, and without warning. He knew he needed additional help, but he'd crossed an invisible threshold where a door slammed behind him, and he was immersed in darkness. The depression wrapped around him like a coarse blanket, and it told him he was unworthy and less than human. He fought it as long as he could."

I sat still and pained on the love seat, tears clouding the view of my clenched hands. The medium allowed me some time to sit with Kent's words. I knew the words to be true, but wasn't expecting this admission or what came next.

"I have another message," Caroline said. With humor in her voice, "Kent says, on a much lighter note, did you decaffeinate yourself?"

"What?" I managed a small laugh, "Yes, I decaffeinated myself. The coffee gave me terrible shakes and jitters in the morning. It made typing difficult. I haven't told a soul about getting off the caffeine. How did he know?"

"Loved ones like to check up on us from time to time, to see how we are doing," Caroline said. "Kent says he doesn't know how you did it. He could never have given up his coffee."

"I believe that. He adored coffee and had several cups throughout the day, which often included runs to Starbucks."

Caroline continued, "At times, he likes to lie next to you at night to bring you comfort, but he says it's crowded. He has to move something out of the way. Do you have a pet?"

I nodded. "I do have a cat. It's funny, even as a kitten, she took to sleeping on what used to be Kent's side of the bed, so having to move her makes sense."

"Did Kent like to tinker with tools and such? It looks as though it may have been a hobby."

"Uh-huh," was all I could get out, feeling a bit shell-shocked.

"He's admitting he wasn't very good at it. He would get frustrated and just walk away from projects."

"That's true," I said. "He could get very frustrated and have mini-temper tantrums. Working with tools and saws just wasn't his thing, though he did try."

"It feels like Kent had a great sense of humor," Caroline said as she pushed some wayward hair out of her face, "very self deprecating. The humor was what drew you to him. He's laughing, saying he doesn't know how you put up with him at times."

That had been easy. It felt like Kent was in the room with me and we were speaking directly. The feeling was warm, and one I didn't want to end, but it did.

"Kent's stepping away to allow another spirit to come forward. It's a man who was very good with numbers, with formulaic math. The man is giving me the image of a metal compass he used. I don't know if anyone still uses this item, it looks archaic."

I shook my head. "I have no idea who that is." I did know that spirits showed up for a reason. It took a lot of energy for them to link with a medium, and they connected with purpose. So I was frustrated that I couldn't name this person.

"It's common for clients to go 'brain dead' during a session, and not recognize a loved one. Don't worry about it, you may remember who the person is later, when you get home."

Little did I know, it would take a year and a heart-wrenching event to learn that spirit's identity.

The medium took a drink from the bottled water that had been sitting next to her chair and placed it back on the floor. "Is there anyone else you might like to connect with?"

"Can you try to reach Susan?" I asked.

"Did you work with Susan?"

Again, how did she know that? "Yes, we worked together."

"She's showing me an office setting and she's sitting behind a desk. She gives me the image of an octopus, where she's feverishly multi-tasking. Susan is very glad to not be doing that work any longer. She liked it for a time, but not at the end. She would smile and put on a brave face for others, but you were the only one she confided in."

I nodded. Susan had been my best friend, boss, and mentor. I missed her, and still pictured her in her old office at work. She had helped me immeasurably when Kent passed. It had been unimaginable that I would lose my best friend on the heels of losing my husband.

Caroline said, "She's letting me know she fought hard not to leave. Susan was not a quitter. I'm given this feeling when someone dies of cancer."

I bowed my head, fighting the tears. "She had ovarian cancer, and she fought it with all she had for two years."

"I'm seeing a young woman, possibly her daughter, that may have participated in a cancer walk in her name. Susan is showing me she was there, traveling along side her during the event. Does that make sense?"

"Yes, I also participated in the walk/run for Ovarian Cancer. I walked it, but her daughter ran.

The family and friends all wore T-shirts with Susan's picture across their chests. It was bittersweet."

"Please let Susan's daughter know her mother was with her every step of the way, and she appreciated how she was remembered."

"I will. I'm sure her daughter would love to know her mother was with her."

Caroline indicated that our hour was about up, and asked if I had any further questions. I did. "Can you tell me about my career?"

"I often consult with Archangel Gabriel on matters of careers, as well as your guides and angels." She paused for an instant. "Are you retired for two years or do you plan to retire in two years? I keep getting two years."

Amazing. "I've just recently been talking about retiring in two years, that's my goal."

"Kent says you will be fine. He's happy for you and says you deserve it, you've worked so hard," Caroline said.

The medium cocked her head to one side, like a bird sensing a worm. "I'm being given that you are a writer. You also have the ability to see where a person's life is out of balance, and you offer suggestions that people listen to, and take to heart. You may do some work as a life coach or counselor."

"Hmmm," I said. I wasn't sure about either of those observations, but I did have one final question.

"Can you tell me about my own intuitive abilities?"

Caroline appeared to be listening to someone and then looked at me. "I sense you have a well-developed intuitive spirit and that you are empathic, especially with your daughter. I believe using tarot cards would be a great way for you to expand your intuition. There are so many beautiful decks to work with."

My gut tightened at the mention of tarot cards. A tiny spark ignited and a low burn began in my belly. I had no idea what that was about, since I knew nothing of the tarot.

My session ended. I paid Caroline and thanked her again for the reading. She let me know she would put a CD of our session in the mail to me within days.

I arrived home, but had no memory of the drive, the roads, or the scenery. My thoughts careened around my mind like a pinball. I sat unmoving on my sofa, holding my head, emotionally exhausted from the conversations and memories of loved ones. I was unsettled, but found the reading experience to be fascinating. I was so relieved to connect with Kent, and to learn he had created his own bit of heaven. When alive, he'd told me that watching the sunrise while floating upon our nearby lake was a spiritual experience for him, a place he felt closest to God. Knowing he was doing that in spirit was comforting.

I was glad I had booked the appointment with Caroline, but I fought to wrap my head around her suggestion to work with tarot cards. I would need to give that idea more thought, but was intrigued, and wondered why I had reacted physically. What I didn't realize at the time was that Caroline's reading was a destiny point on my soul journey, an unseen course correction. I was a passenger on a train that suddenly switched to a different track. This new fork would take me to places and introduce me to people I could have never imagined.

2

The First of Many

The psychic medium's reading kept playing over in my head like a song from the radio. I repeatedly pictured Kent's heaven, him being on water, and at peace.

His love of water had been a constant, like the dark brown color of his eyes. When our daughter was a toddler, my husband surprised me by purchasing two canary-yellow kayaks. Since we lived near a river and five small lakes, it made perfect sense, and he said it would be fun for our date nights. He was right. (I'm sure his interest in fishing played some small part in the plan.)

We paddled our way into many wondrous memories that live with me to this day. Sightings of hawks, turkey vultures, deer and coyotes were treasured while we ventured along the Cosumnes River in our kayaks.

One frightening experience, different from the norm, happened at a nearby lake at dusk. An eerie time to be in the wild; a changing of the guard could be felt in the muted light. Animals that had been busy all day scurried to their homes, while others were just waking to begin their activities under the cover of darkness.

We had been on the lake for more than an hour, and our excursion was at end. I dipped the oar into the water and took a few strokes, and felt a small vibration as the front of my kayak scraped against the shallow bottom. Kent was close behind. As I climbed out of the kayak and stepped into the muddied lake-bed, I glimpsed movement out of the corner of my eye. A kingsnake, slithered across the water, keen on its destination. A scream escaped my mouth worthy of a horror flick. Kent, seeing my tormentor, let out a hearty laugh. I had no idea snakes were skilled at swimming. Rushing out of the water, I squinted into the darkness for anything else that might be trying to make a move towards me. It took some time for my fear to subside and for my heart to return to its normal cadence.

That incident aside, our confidence in manning the kayaks grew. Kent planned an ocean adventure to our favorite place, Pacific Grove, California. We loved the small-town feel, and that we could walk to the ocean from our bed and breakfast. We had traveled to Pacific Grove many times, alone and with our children. I couldn't wait to go back.

Since this was our first kayak venture into rougher waters, my nerves started to get the best of me. While driving to our destination, apprehension weaved its way through my stomach. I tried to push my fears aside and looked out the window at the beautiful scenery. Blue skies and great weather helped calm me.

We parked near Lovers Point, and unleashed the kayaks from the roof-rack on Kent's SUV. We carried the boats down countless steps, struggling as we made our way to the beach. Out of breath, we set our cargo down on the sand at water's edge and rested. I closed my eyes and filled my lungs with the fresh salt air. Being near any great body of water always restored me, but I wasn't quite sure if navigating it would have the same effect.

Kent broke into my reverie. "Are you ready?"

Gazing up at my love, I said, "I am now." He held out a hand to help me up and I kissed him on the lips in thanks. I stepped into the water and then into the kayak. I scooted my legs down into the hull and held my oar across my chest at the ready.

Kent gave me a hard push that sent sprays of salt water into my face. I paddled furiously to get beyond the incoming waves, and Kent was beside me in short order. The breeze played with his salt and pepper hair, and he wore a look of pure joy, an emotion that rarely graced his face.

Kent took the lead and headed towards a large rock formation where seals, cormorants, and sea gulls were sunning themselves. Being close to nature was a mutual love, and one of our many bonds. Watching creatures in their natural habitat kept us spellbound. Both of us absorbed the sights and sounds of the ocean as we bobbed up and down. We kept a respectful distance, not wanting to scare the seals and birds off their precious real estate.

Kent told me he wanted to explore some other areas, and I watched him glide away. Spying an otter, I paddled towards it. As I drew near, I was astounded to find seven otters in a semicircle, wrapped in kelp and perfectly spaced, as if gems on a necklace. They had twirled themselves into the brown kelp like string around a yoyo. They rested peacefully on their backs, and exerted no energy to stay put. I, on the other hand, struggled. The wind pushed me into their solitude, and I grabbed and held the slimy seaweed to keep my vantage point. That worked for a minute, but then another gust tried to take my oar out to sea, and I snatched it at the last second. I pulled the oar in close to my body, and leaned up and over it, using my breasts to lock it in place. I dropped both hands into the frigid water and wrapped seaweed around my wrists to keep my spot. A picture of me hunched over, boobs securing the oar, arms handcuffed by kelp, wouldn't make the cover of the National Geographic. The image was better suited for Mad Magazine.

I looked for Kent; I wanted to share the moment, but he was too far away. When I glanced back to the otters, I noticed several staring at me. They seemed to be deciding whether I was friend or foe. To put them at ease, I started singing, "The wheels on the bus go round and round, round and round, round and round..." My daughter's nursery song was the only melody that came to mind. It seemed to work as they settled down, and some closed their eyes, paws nestled together, as if in prayer. Most likely asking God to stop my singing.

Kent called my name. Releasing one of my kelp anchors, I pivoted and put my palm up and signaled him to slow down, then I put my forefinger to my lips to indicate silence. He came to a slow stop next to me, his eyes fixed on the otters. He whispered, "I wondered who the hell you were singing to, I would never have guessed this audience. How long have you been here?"

"For quite a while now. Isn't it something?"

We floated in silence, relishing the rare opportunity before us.

Singing to the otters at Lovers Point is a treasured memory. My final recollection of Lovers Point happened years after the first, and it haunts me. It began at home, with an urgent knock at our front door. The loud noise frightened Katie, our eleven year old daughter. She came into my bathroom like a rocket, saying something I couldn't make out. I turned off the blow dryer. In a breathless voice she said, "Someone has been pounding at the front door, didn't you hear it?"

"No, I've been trying to dry my hair," I said, waving the dryer. *Who could it be at 9:30 p.m.?* Katie knew we did not get visitors at bedtime. Hair wet, I went to the door in flannel pajamas and slippers. I turned on the porch light and peered into the peep hole. I saw Bob, my daughter's softball coach, shifting from side-to-side. A great guy who also happened to be a police detective. Bob and my husband worked at the Sacramento Police Department, Kent as the Facilities Manager. I opened the door, and noticed a second man behind Bob. The man's stiff white collar blinded me: *a man of the cloth.* I wanted this gentleman off my porch. My body became rigid, as I repeated,

"No Bob, No Bob . . . " I fought the urge to cover my ears. Instincts told me I didn't want to hear the news he'd come to deliver.

This sudden event thrust me into a horrible movie, the one where a cop and a clergyman darken an unsuspecting person's front door. Whenever that tag-team appeared, it never went well for the individual answering their knock. But I was not in a theater and the two men still stood before me, looking grim.

I became aware of Katie glued to my side, arms tight around my waist. I attempted to regain some composure for her sake. I tilted her chin up to look at me. "Please go to your room; I have to talk to Bob. I'll come and get you in a little bit."

"Why can't I stay?"

"I need you to go to your room and not give me any trouble right now. I promise I'll come get you in a few minutes." She unhooked herself from my side, and headed down the hallway. Once I heard her bedroom door close, I showed the two men to the family room.

They sat on the sofa and I sat across from them on the love seat. Bob introduced me to the chaplain, but I didn't hear his name. I stared blankly, trying to grasp my own scattered thoughts. *Kent is in Pacific Grove, getting away for a few days. What could have happened? Was he involved in a car accident?*

A heart attack or stroke? My mind sped through the possibilities.

Bob cleared his throat and brought me back. He said, "I received a call this evening from the Monterey County Police Department. I'm so sorry, Erin, I'm here to tell you that Kent was found dead this morning."

Dead? The room whirled and I put my hands on the love seat to steady myself. Light headed and sobbing, I said, "I just . . . spoke to him . . . yesterday. Are you sure it's him?"

Bob nodded. "A jogger spotted his body in the ocean and notified police. They found his car later; keys and driver's license inside, along with letters he left for family, and empty pill bottles. His kayak also washed up. It appears he took sedatives, put his kayak in at Lovers Point, and drowned himself."

This can't be happening. I spoke to him yesterday and he sounded fine. He can't be gone. I sat in the family room with these two men, yet I drifted far outside my body, floating, taking in this strange scene. My sense of desperation made me want to escape this place and go back in time, to alter what had transpired between us.

I recalled the painful day Kent and I separated. A year and a half prior to our parting, Kent had suffered an injury to his back while at work. It had started out a day like any other. He went off to work and returned home. When he came in, he told me he had lifted something heavy and wrenched his back. He shuffled into the bedroom, bent forward at the waist, hand on his lower back. "I'm going to take some ibuprofen and rest a bit." He saw my concern and tried to smile, but it came out as a grimace.

It was not the first time Kent had carried home aches and pains from work. Somehow, he always managed to heal, so this latest episode didn't seem significant. In hindsight, a terrifying alarm like a tornado warning should have been shattering my eardrums. That day marked the beginning of the end to many things I cherished.

My husband's back pain grew worse. He resisted being put on medications. He knew it was never a good thing for a recovering alcoholic, an addictive personality, to take prescribed drugs. He succumbed to the drugs when his suffering became too great. The torture of his back prevented him from doing many things he loved, like boating, fishing and hiking. The world he had known shrank.

After many agonizing months, Kent had back surgery. We had hoped this would be the solution to his nightmare. It wasn't. The doctor declared the surgery a success, but Kent had a different opinion. His pain remained, and it joined his ever-growing fury. The Workers Comp doctor gave him two things: a release to return to work, and a prescription to manage his pain.

My husband hadn't been himself for some time. It was more than his depression and back. Something else lurked beneath the surface. I questioned him. "What's wrong honey?"

"Nothing, I'm just tired."

Kent kept me at arm's length. I found his behavior distressing, and unusual. We'd always been very close, sharing our burdens and working on issues as a team. He began to treat me like an opponent, and I didn't understand why.

Another changed behavior occurred in the way he entered our home from work. Kent used to greet Katie and me with huge smiles, hugs, and kisses. He would change into comfy clothes and want to hear all about our day. He often took Katie swimming, or he'd fish before dinner. Now he barely mustered a hello, and often said he had to take a nap. With a slight limp, he would make his way into the bedroom and close the door. Katie and I would eat dinner, do homework, and get ready for bed. As I tucked the covers around our daughter, Kent would emerge from his "nap," and head to the kitchen for some dinner. His days and nights turned upside down.

At first I feared he might be drinking again, but I couldn't smell or read any signs of alcohol. I knew he had a 30 day supply of his prescription for pain. I wondered if he had forgotten when he had taken his last pill, and had taken another by mistake. Taking the pills too closely together might explain the strange behavior and the slurring of words. When I asked if he had taken his medication as directed, he became enraged. That should have been a clue.

One awful weekend he stayed in bed, saying he didn't feel well. I wanted to go to the emergency room because he appeared so listless. "Let me take you to the hospital."

"No, I'll go on Monday if I'm not better," he mumbled.

Katie and I were committed to work a carnival for her sixth grade overnight trip, so we were in and out of the house. Kent had known about our weekend obligation for some time, but now our being gone angered him.

When Katie and I got home Sunday night, the bedroom door was closed, so I assumed Kent was sleeping. Within moments, he burst out of the bedroom and yelled, "I can't take it anymore!" and stormed out. For the life of me, I didn't know what it was he couldn't take anymore. I stood frozen, thinking he would walk back in, but he didn't.

He left the night before Katie was to start her first day of sixth grade. His job had been to get Katie off to school in the mornings, and mine was to pick her up in the evenings. I had to call my boss and let her know I would be late to work, since I now needed to get Katie to school.

Kent stayed gone for a week. I still had no idea what had upset him, but by then I didn't care. Anger had replaced concern. He had left me to deal with the responsibilities of the house and our daughter, all on my own. During the week we were apart I noticed a difference in the house: the energy felt much lighter. With the brooding dark cloud absent, I realized I wasn't walking on eggshells.

In the peace of that week, my anger subsided and I came to a painful realization that tore at my heart. I couldn't continue living the way I had. My husband looked like the man I married, but he didn't act like him. I could put up with his crazy sleeping pattern, but I couldn't handle the absence of the kind and nurturing person I'd always known. That man lay hidden. Anger and rage came much too easily to him now. Kent wasn't himself, and talking and questioning did nothing. My husband had disappeared within himself, and I couldn't find a way to reach him and pull him out. And even more frustrating I knew he kept a secret.

He wanted to return home after being gone a week, but I told him I wanted a separation. A torturous conversation ensued. At the end of it, we cried and held each other, and agreed we needed time apart.

I hoped and prayed he would seek help for what troubled him. That he might return to counseling or seek something, other than drugs, to manage his back pain. I didn't speak of divorce; I still loved my husband. I just wanted the humorous and charismatic man I had married to come back to me.

During our six months apart, we still spoke to one another and co-parented. We attended all of Katie's sporting events, and celebrated Christmas with our kids at the house. Instead of getting better and seeking help, he seemed more "out of it." His grown kids noticed it, too. Katie had recently told me that she didn't want to stay at his condo because he would fall asleep, or forget to feed her. She had to remind him they hadn't eaten.

When young, Kent had battled addiction and depression; he had first tried to take his life at the age of nineteen. Now, at 55, he had years of experience with antidepressants. He'd always led me to believe he knew how to manage his private pain and sorrow. He had successfully fought to keep his demons at bay for over 35 years. Kent had enjoyed his life and kids for a very long time. I had been lulled into a sense of safety, and never dreamt that taking his own life could be an option. I believed his overriding love for his children tethered him to this earth. I had no idea how far he had fallen into the abyss.

The chaplain stood up. I had been so lost in thought, I had forgotten that he and Bob were still in the room. Like a splash of frigid water, it hit me again why they were there.

"May I use your restroom?" the chaplain asked.

"Yes, it's straight down the hall."

I met Bob's gaze. "I need to get Katie."

I steeled myself. I was grateful the two men had stayed while I told Katie that her father had taken his own life. I wrapped my arms around her slender body, as she shuddered and cried. I ached for the both of us. I told her the truth about her father because I didn't want Kent's suicide to be a family secret, or something shameful. His pain and his choices needed to see the light of day, so all could heal and forgive.

Telling my daughter and my step-kids about the death of their father was heart-wrenching. Just as tormenting were the calls to Kent's siblings. I'm sure I made many mistakes in dealing with the intricacies of Kent's death. Unfortunately, I knew of no primer that could guide me through it. I followed my heart and my moral compass. My top priorities were protecting Kent's children and respecting his final wishes.

While retrieving Kent's belongings and cleaning his condo, I uncovered the secret he had kept hidden. He had become addicted to pain medications. Not being able to get them from his own doctor, he had resorted to ordering them off the Internet from Canada. He had them shipped to a co-worker's house at first, and then to his condo. I found that some drugs had made it across the border to him, and some had been seized by the government. Penalties were rendered only if he tried to claim the confiscated prescriptions. I learned of his secret much too late.

Kent and I had been together for sixteen years. I had no idea how difficult it would be to live in a world without him in it. I had enjoyed our marriage and the love we'd shared for a long time, and it saddened me the last two years had been so challenging. I wished I could have helped him recover from his latest addiction, but I knew that I was powerless to make him get clean and sober. Overcoming drug and alcohol addiction was always an inside job.

When Kent died, I was in love with him. I was left with a heart full of feelings and I didn't know what to do with them. I couldn't touch or see the person that they belonged to. There was an abrupt stop to the flow of them. They swam around inside me, looking for their home, but it was gone.

Little did I know that Kent would be the first of many loved ones who would take their leave. The last time I had lost a family member, I had been a young girl, and I hadn't understood the ramifications. With Kent's death, I fully comprehended the finality and loneliness in store for me. Grief moved in and stayed. Even on sunny days I could feel it and see it. Grief became my shadow.

I was not alone in my feelings; all our family had been affected by Kent's death. Anguish enveloped us, it took many years to reassemble our hearts. But the pieces never quite go back the same.

It's All in the Cards

A small notion crept into my being and took hold. That small notion was Caroline's suggestion of using tarot cards to expand my intuition. I'd had a physical reaction when she suggested them during my recent reading. *What was it about the cards that triggered me?* I knew nothing of the tarot, nor did I know if it was possible to grow one's intuition.

In the weeks and months that followed, my thoughts never wandered far from Caroline's strange recommendation. My stomach went a little hinky when I contemplated immersing myself in the tarot.

The first challenge to overcome was the stigma and ridicule that seemed to go hand-in-hand with people involved in the psychic world. If I got involved with the tarot, I would be throwing open a door and sending out an open invitation for contempt. I didn't even like the word psychic. I preferred the word intuitive. "Psychic" conjured up sketchy images from B movies, where someone predicted less than fabulous futures for unwitting souls. That was not me, and that was not something I wanted to be associated with. My interest in the cards was to expand my intuition, and to possibly help others. If I was to get involved with this endeavor, I would need to revamp my preconceived notions and make peace with the word psychic.

I was not in the habit of being hassled for my beliefs, or being the brunt of jokes. Yet I knew that was a real threat. Some tarot readers and psychics were belittled for their practices. If I invested myself in the psychic realm, I would need to toughen up, and sprout alligator skin to deal with the criticisms I was sure to face. Much of what I wanted to explore was too woo-woo for many, family included. I knew some relatives would think I had lost all my marbles, yet others would be kind enough to assist in the search of them.

Adding to my apprehension was a secret desire to talk to dead people. *Was that even possible for someone like me, a regular working mom?* I hadn't read any accounts of individuals who had embarked on mediumship at my advanced age; most had known of their abilities when young, or their gifts awakened from a near-death experience. I let my guides know that I was fine with not having a near-death experience. I was more than willing to put in the time and labor to grow my intuition, slowly, if need be. I'd felt intuitive throughout my life, always calling it "my gut," but I couldn't recall any instance of talking to spirits or seeing them. There was no template for what I was hoping to accomplish.

My one ray of hope was John Holland, a psychic medium. I'd read he'd grown up in an alcoholic home, so I connected to him on that level. He had been aware of his abilities his whole life, and he spoke of using tarot cards and psychometry. One day, after having done psychic readings for years, a female spirit showed up. The apparition sat next to the woman he was reading. It was the first time he communicated directly to spirit. He passed on the message from spirit, to the woman receiving the reading. I hoped that if I opened up and developed through tarot cards, one day, I might have a similar experience.

I investigated mediums, psychics, and tarot readers. I learned many of my earlier prejudices were not based on reality, and that there were many earnest and caring individuals who were practicing their psychic abilities. Their intent was to help others and heal those who had been wounded from the loss of a loved one. Most wanted to share that there was something beyond our physical life, and that our souls were eternal. They were into Source/Universe/God's white light, accurate messages, and positive intentions. That was me, and what I desired to bring to tarot card readings. If any other abilities developed while working with the cards, so be it.

Getting beyond my jitters and worries was necessary, that much I understood. Fear could become a block to receiving spirit messages, so moving beyond what other people thought was paramount. I needed the liberty to voice what came to me intuitively, even though it made no sense to me. I had to remain steadfast if someone thought me nutty. Stone by stone, I would need to build a fortress of certainty.

After weeks of prayer and careful consideration, weighing pros and cons, and desires, I came to a decision. I would not only learn how to read tarot cards, but would practice any positive suggestions on ways to connect with spirit. It felt like I was embarking on an exciting adventure, making my way up a gangway to a luxury ship, getting ready to sail to uncharted destinations. I hadn't felt this enthused in years. *So where to start?*

While devouring many books and doing loads of Internet research, one theme rose to the top: meditation. I had heard about meditating for years, but I resisted it, not wanting to add one more thing to my daily "to do" list. The tired Mom within was hoping to bypass this step, but it appeared to be a necessary component to receive messages. The belief was that one needed to quiet the mind to hear and see the subtle communications from one's higher self, guides or spirit. In my everyday life, my mind raced with rapid-fire thoughts of work and home responsibilities. Spirit would be hard-pressed to break through my raucous ruminations. There was so much racket, I couldn't hear my own thoughts, let alone a message. No longer able to avoid it, I would have to pull up my big girl pants and start a daily practice of meditation.

Picking a consistent time and quiet place to meditate each day had been advised. Not only would that encourage the habit, it would let spirit know that I'd made a commitment to the practice. It created a sacred time for us to connect. Because of my job, our special time would have to be in the evenings before I went to bed. I could not drag myself awake, blurry-eyed, any earlier than my current 4:50 a.m. start time.

The next task on my psychic quest was to find a deck of tarot cards. I was hoping my guides and intuition would kick-in. I got online and delved into the world of the tarot.

It appeared the exact origin of the tarot was unknown, but decks were dated as far back as the 1400s in Europe. Tarot cards used for divination dated back to the 1500s. A current deck used by many was the Rider-Waite deck. It consisted of 78 cards. The Major Arcana (greater secrets) had 22 cards that depicted themes or spiritual lessons that were playing out in the sitter's (the person getting the reading) life. The Minor Arcana (lesser secrets) had 56 cards that included four suits represented by coins (earth), wands (fire), cups (water) and swords (air). The four suits depicted what might be happening in a sitter's everyday life. There were also court cards: Pages, Knights, Queens and Kings, that might reflect characters involved in a person's life. If I learned the Rider-Waite deck first, all of the other tarot decks would be easier because they had similar formats.

Wanting to experience the cards up close, to feel them in my own hands, I searched for local metaphysical stores. I took a drive up Highway 50. While walking through the store, I witnessed various readers sitting at small tables, mixed in amongst the merchandise. I wondered what it would be like to do a reading so exposed? Were sitters okay with other customers milling about hearing their personal business?

As I strolled through the store, the beautiful colors of crystals, rocks, singing bowls, and clothes caught my eye. The smell of incense wafted about the room.

"May I help you?" A grey-haired saleswoman inquired.

"I'd like to look at some tarot decks."

With a wave of her hand she gestured for me to follow her to the back of the store. She stepped behind a glass case and jangled a set of keys. She found the one she was looking for and opened the sliding panel. I pointed to a few decks, and she grabbed the boxes, and placed them on top of the glass. The saleswoman then excused herself to help another customer.

I scrutinized the artwork of each deck, hoping for some mysterious signal, but nothing happened. The images didn't speak to me or, as some would say, turn me on. I had read that it was important to "connect" with the cards. Some decks were illustrated with fairies and gnomes, and those creatures, though interesting, didn't resonate with me. I couldn't picture myself giving a serious reading using that cast of characters. Other decks had words written under the painted artwork, such as "Love" or "Loss," while others had no words, just beautifully drawn images, so intuition would play a much greater role. Selecting a deck was a matter of personal taste, and unfortunately, I didn't receive a nudge to buy any of them.

Back home, I got online and explored sites that sold tarot cards. There were too many choices, but there was one deck that grabbed me. It was The Psychic Tarot Oracle Deck by John Holland. It was different from the Rider-Waite deck in that it had fewer cards, 65 total, and there were no court cards. It did include seven chakra cards that reflected the main energy centers of the body. The artwork captivated me, and the more I considered the deck, the more I knew that my tarot journey must begin with these cards. With a click of the mouse, I ordered them.

When my purchase arrived in the mail, I was like a kid at Christmas. I tore into the package and dived into the box to find an instruction guide and the tarot cards. I loved the detailed drawings, and the many beautiful colors. The back of the cards wore a rich purple hue and were trimmed in gold. The center design had an array of gold circles, many of them overlapped and connected. I lovingly rubbed the cards.

The guidebook gave many suggestions: how to care for the cards, how to get to know them, and encouraged a person to interpret them in their own fashion. Make the cards your own. The booklet accompanying the cards was only meant to be a jumping-off point.

My commitment to meditation and the tarot began in earnest. I meditated most days, and pulled cards to study. It took many months to feel comfortable with the tarot, and soon I couldn't wait to feel the weight of the deck in my hands. Different feelings were evoked when I handled the cards, special feelings. Additional meanings, other than what was offered in the guidebook, would come to me so a card would gain several expressions. What was going on in my personal life seemed to attach itself to the graphic designs, and my knowledge of the cards expanded. Once I felt comfortable with The Psychic Tarot Oracle Deck, I felt compelled to learn the Rider-Waite deck. After mastering two decks, I jokingly told others I was now bilingual.

Meditation proved a little harder to nail down. I had to experiment for months before I found a practice that worked. There was an abundance of information on how to meditate and the reading of some of it made me sleepy. Not the desired effect. I tried: guided meditations, sitting in silence, breath work, and listening to instrumental music. In the beginning, my mind resisted. I was relentless in my daily practice, and eventually earned small victories of quiet. Over time, I settled on a combination of techniques that worked.

My routine started by dancing to music that woke-up my body and raised my vibration. Next I sat in a chair, feet planted on the ground, and prayed while instrumental music played in the background. I thanked God for my blessings, along with my spirit guides, angels and loved ones. I also prayed for signs and symbols from my guides to let me know I was on the right spiritual path. After that, I meditated, incorporating breath work. I got quiet and listened for God and Spirit to inspire. My days were more centered and peaceful when I practiced meditation and pulled tarot cards.

Once I had shifted my focus to a more spiritual life, a strange thing occurred while at work. I walked up a long aisle, like I'd done a million times before, but this time was different. I heard a quiet voice say, *You don't belong here anymore.* I turned to see if someone was speaking to me, but no one was near. The voice had come from within. I thought, *Why don't I belong here anymore?* The message came randomly and repeatedly, always catching me unaware while at work. I'd been praying for a sign, but now that I'd heard a voice, it spooked me.

What I found odd about the message was that I had always considered my office a second home, welcoming and warm. My original plan had been to work for five more years and retire at sixty, but a new seed had been planted. The feeling grew that I didn't belong anymore, and I was supposed to do something else. I had no idea what that something else was, but it wasn't the job I had had for years.

Concurrently, my mom's health was declining. She was in an assisted living facility, and I'd felt torn between my mother and my responsibilities to my employer. I took time off work to take her to her various appointments, but then every time my mom fell she had to be taken to the emergency room, per the rules of the assisted living facility. Then I would need additional time off. A dementia diagnosis came after one of her many falls. My brother and his wife, Laney, had just experienced the effects of dementia on his father, my stepfather, so it was inconceivable that this debilitating condition now claimed our mother.

I made the decision to retire for many reasons. The main one was so I could be available to my mother and not have to ask permission to take her to a medical appointment. I had always been a dependable employee, but missing work made it difficult to maintain that.

I had worked since I was 15 and a half years old, and to not wake to an alarm proved a blessing. I found the opportunity to control my days exhilarating, and I was excited to explore what a non-work life could be. During my first week of independence I became a professional sleeper. I hugged the pillow, and proudly wore crisscrossing sheet-lines upon my face. My sleep-tank had run on empty for years and now I had the luxury to fill it.

Retirement allowed my body clock to return to its natural rhythm. I no longer went to bed at 8:00 p.m. and could now stay up past midnight, if I wanted. The simple joys in life, like reading a book into the wee hours of the night, were cherished. I switched the study of the tarot cards and meditation to the beginning of my day, since I no longer had to work. This earlier start brought added clarity.

With my new-found freedom, I gave myself permission to try new experiences, and sought out like-minded people. I traveled alone and attended the I Can Do It event in Southern California, put on by Hay House Publishing. Many of their best-selling self-help authors were doing presentations. One such author and motivational speaker was Dr. Wayne Dyer. I'd seen him on TV, but was thrilled to see him in person and got to shake his hand. His messages were inspirational.

I also saw two of my favorite psychic mediums, James Van Praagh and John Holland. I was fascinated to watch them work and bring spirit through for several lucky individuals. It invigorated me to be around so many people who openly loved the metaphysical.

I went on an *Awaken Your Spirit* cruise. Workshops were hosted by Sonia Choquette and John Holland, both psychic mediums and spiritual teachers. Later, I took an online tarot class hosted by John Holland and Ann Hentz. Ann, a master tarot instructor, had done readings for 30 years. I was fortunate to get through on the phone lines, and asked about doing readings for others, and told them the three cards I'd pulled for their exercise. Ann Hentz said, "I think you better get out there and do some readings for people! The Temptation Card says your readings are going to help them see where they are held back, where their demons are." John Holland added, "I'm picking up, intuitively, that you're going to give people strong legs to stand on, you're going to give them strength." Buoyed by their encouragement, I started to give tarot readings to family and friends.

I had been asking my guides, angels, and loved ones to give me a sign that I was on the right spiritual path. I became aware that I kept seeing the number 222 everywhere. My birthday is 2/22, so to see that number held special meaning. Seeing 222 became so frequent that I took pictures to prove to my friends, I wasn't making the sightings up. I took photos of my odometer, clocks, signs along the road, cash registers, gasoline pumps and slot machines. I bought Doreen Virtue's "Angel Numbers" book. It said for 222: "Have Faith. Everything's going to be all right. Don't worry about anything, as this situation is resolving itself beautifully for everyone involved." At the time, I worried about two things: was I on an intuitive wild goose chase, and my mother's failing health. It hurt to see her slipping away, becoming someone I didn't know. The angel message calmed me, and each time I saw 222, I was reminded to "Have Faith."

One night, after spending the day with my mother, I was filled with anguish. I pulled out my tarot cards and asked for guidance about my mother's condition. It pained me to see her lie in a bed with no quality of life. I had hoped the tarot could soothe me. I fanned the deck out before me, and with a finger, selected just one card. I flipped it over to reveal the word *Patience*. I knew all was in God's hands and that my mother's fate was entwined with divine timing.

While I contemplated the card, my daughter, Katie, arrived home. She floated into the room, tanned, and wearing a yellow halter top and a long flowing white skirt. She looked at the table and said, "Oh cool, you're pulling cards. Will you pull some for me?"

I told her I was upset about grandma and had asked the cards for some guidance. As she drew close, I held up the Patience card for her to see. Her eyes grew wide. "I don't believe it."

"You don't believe what?"

"I wasn't going to tell you, but now I feel I have

to." Katie bent and pulled her long billowing skirt up to her thigh to reveal a large bandaged area.

"How did you get hurt?"

"I didn't get hurt, I got a tattoo." She gingerly peeled away the bandage to expose the latest artwork etched onto her body. There, emblazoned in bold letters, was the word *Patience*.

I was dumbfounded. *What were the odds?*

"Crazy, huh?" My daughter said. "I wasn't going to tell you, but when I saw that card, I knew I had to show you. Got to go and meet up with some friends." And with a quick hug, she vanished.

I believe once you adjust your focus and start to see the signs, more will come to you. It's as though your guides and angels know you are finally understanding their language. My guides were busy working to give me the signs I had asked for. They were making me a believer.

Another instance occurred while I traveled Highway 99 to a medical appointment. I had my favorite radio station on, and was cruising at 70 miles per hour. I glanced left at a huge electronic billboard. An advertisement flashed on the screen: "The Lives We Touch Inspire Us," at the same time the radio blurted, "The Lives We Touch Inspire Us," in perfect syncopation to the voice in my head!

I couldn't say what the ad was for, I just knew my spirit guides were at work and I wasn't alone.

The rest of my trip was driven in stunned silence. I couldn't wait to tell my friends of this latest occurrence, and I definitely had more to add to my psychic journal.

I contacted the radio station and asked what commercial had come on the air at 1:10 p.m. The gal on the other end of the phone said she had to check. When she got back on the line she said it was an ad for a children's hospital. Their tag line was "The Lives We Touch Inspire Us." I thanked her. I also thanked my guides.

A short while after that event, I reread "Trust Your Vibes" by Sonia Choquette. In it, she talked of living a sixth sensory life. I had already made the commitment to live a sixth sensory life, I just needed a refresher course. In her book, she suggested doing creative things to use the right side of your brain to become more intuitive. I loved coloring as a child, and thought that would be a positive creative outlet. So I jumped into my car, and headed off to Hobby Lobby for coloring books for adults and felt-tip pens.

I grabbed a shopping cart and headed to the rear of the store while passing row after row of merchandise. I stopped at an ocean-themed display of knick-knacks and small figures. *Why are you stopping here? You don't even like knick-knacks.* As a kid, I loathed having to dust all of my grandmother's ceramic statues. That chore swore me off collecting anything, especially figurines, but something drew me to the nautical-themed wonderland. I had just recommitted myself to living a sixth sensory life, now here I was back to my old self, with my logic fighting my intuition.

I decided to just go with it, and asked, *Why did you stop here?* My eyes drifted over the items on the shelves and landed on a bronzed sea turtle. I heard, *That's it.* I said, "Fine," to no one in particular, and placed the damn thing in my cart. I had no idea why I was supposed to buy the little dust collector, but it was going home with me. I finally reached my original destination and found some wonderful adult coloring books and a big box-set of felt pens. Now I had the tools to go home and be creative.

When I got home, I placed the sea turtle on a book shelf in the living room and promptly forgot about it.

One month later I was texting with my sister-in-law, Laney. She and my brother were on a boat in Hawaii. An image came into my third eye chakra, my internal screen. I saw a black and white picture of my brother snorkeling with his arm outstretched, chasing a sea turtle. I did something unusual, I didn't keep the sighting to myself. I quickly texted Laney and told her to pass on a message to my brother. "Tell him to say hi to the sea turtle for me."

Twenty minutes later my brother texted me. He had been snorkeling and was led on a merry chase by a sea turtle. He followed it for over 15 minutes. When he climbed back into the boat to share the experience with his wife, he was greeted with the words, "Your sister says to say hello to the sea turtle."

Eddy wanted to know how I knew about the turtle. I texted back that I had just received an image of it.

Three weeks later I was packing for a visit to see Eddy and Laney. I passed my bookshelf and my eyes glimpsed the forgotten sea turtle. It hit me; I was supposed to buy it for my brother. I was sure my mom's spirit and my guides had been instrumental, and drew me to the display at Hobby Lobby. The sea turtle was to commemorate Eddy's amazing snorkeling adventure in Hawaii. It was also an exercise in trusting my intuition. I picked up the sea turtle and wrapped it so it could go to its rightful owner.

When I presented the gift to my brother, he just stared at it, not saying a word. I told him the Hobby Lobby story, and showed him the receipt and the date of purchase. I bought the bronzed sea turtle one month prior to his trip to Hawaii. I told him I believed it was from Mom. He thanked me for the gift, but had to add, "You know I don't believe in this kind of stuff. It's just too 'out there' for me."

"I know," I said.

Taking The Plunge

After reading the tarot for friends, their friends, relatives, and anyone else I could coax, the time seemed right to take my readings to the next level. I decided to take the plunge and do readings for the public. The thought alone had the power to both make me sweat, and elevate my heart rate.

The logical place to begin would be at fairs and festivals. I traveled to several local events to get a feel for them, and to learn what readers put into their booths. I searched for a fair that felt comfortable, had great energy, and where I could visualize myself conducting readings.

I had no concept of what one had to do to participate in a festival, or how to market myself. I needed to know what tools were necessary for this new landscape.

It took a week, but I gathered my courage and placed a call to Prasanna, the owner of the Healing Arts Festival. She was very helpful and sent me some preliminary information through email. I learned that before I could purchase a space at the festival, I needed to meet a requirement. I had to give Prasanna a tarot reading. She asked this of all new readers to her show. It was her form of quality control, and it assured customers had access to experienced practitioners.

Prasanna came to my house for our scheduled appointment. As she entered, she greeted me with a smile, but it did nothing to quiet my nerves. Too much rode on this reading. I'd heaped undue pressure on myself, and I was like a tea kettle ready to blow. Doing an "interview" reading created a different energy vibration, and it wasn't pleasant. Feeling as though cotton balls had invaded my mouth, I said, "I'm so nervous."

"Oh, don't be," Prasanna said. "I don't bite and I'm sure you'll do fine."

Not convinced, I showed her to my reading room. Prasanna took a seat at the table. She glanced around, taking note of the artwork, a Buddha on one wall and a mosaic glass-tiled dragonfly on another. A rug, in various shades of blue, rested beneath our feet.

I began with a silent prayer to my higher power and spirit guides. I asked that the session be protected, and that it be for our highest good. I requested only spirits that walked in God's white light draw near to assist with the reading.

Prasanna asked her question of the cards, and made her selection. I scanned them to take in their messages. The reading was a blur, however, I was able to fight my jitters and get into a zone to interpret her cards.

After the reading, I let out my breath. "So what do you think?"

Prasanna's smile lit her face. "You are welcome to be a vendor at my festival."

Clapping my hands together, I shouted, "Oh, thank goodness."

Prasanna laughed. "You know, there is a purpose behind me getting a reading from each newcomer to my show. I've had several experiences where the person read directly from the instruction manual, stating the meaning of the cards. That would not do at my event. I encouraged those readers to gain more experience, and contact me once they no longer needed the manual. I want experienced readers at my show."

"I'm glad I passed the test."

I asked many questions regarding the different size booths, about taking payment from customers, and how to create a space. She had worked as a healer herself, so shared her own experiences working fairs. There was an easy comfort between us, and it felt like we had been friends for years. As she left, Prasanna said, "The next Healing Arts Festival is less than six months away. The time will go by fast." My timeframe was set and the clock began to tick.

What size space should I purchase? I was a bit claustrophobic, so I put painters' tape on my family room floor, and marked off the various sizes to get a visual. I was like Goldilocks; the 6' X 8' booth was too small, and not private enough for my liking. The 10' X 12' was too large. The 10' X 10' felt just right.

I had a painting in my head of what I wanted my booth to look like. To create my artwork, I needed to incorporate the color purple. It was supposed to be a peaceful and spiritual color. I selected a rich dark lavender tablecloth for my greeting table, where business cards and sign-up sheets would be placed. My girlfriend, Diana, stitched a tablecloth to cover my round tarot table. The violet material shimmered, and was smooth to the touch. Emerald green tassels dangled along its edge.

I worked on the wording and design for a six foot professional banner. My "brand" was a hummingbird over a lotus flower, and my business cards reflected the same motif.

Wanting to create a safe haven for sitters, I purchased two privacy screens to complete the look.

Tearing a page off the calendar, I noticed I had one week until my first Healing Arts Festival. Within that week, I practiced encouraging self-talks, as self-doubt and terror crept in. The idea of doing public tarot readings had sounded great six months earlier, but now I wondered what had possessed me. *What if nothing came to me during a reading? What if I bombed?* Pesky thoughts kept darting into my brain, and I had to shoo them away like flies.

A few days before the festival, something unexpected came my way. Prasanna was contacted by a woman who wanted to book a Sunday reading with me. I worried I wouldn't do one tarot reading, and here I was blessed with a booking prior to the event. *Who would have thunk it?* On Cloud 9, I believed my guides had masterminded the event.

The Healing Arts Festival was held at the Scottish Rite Masonic Center, in my hometown, near my alma mater – C.S.U. Sacramento. I observed the banners for the event fluttering in the breeze as I pulled into the tree-lined parking lot. I loaded my gear onto my rolling cart and made my way into the building. I was stunned to see the expanse of the hall, I hadn't remembered it being so large. I located my 10′ X 10′ area and began to create my home for the next two days. Bit by bit, the wide open space grew to a small city of vendors. The din and energy of the room vibrated throughout my body.

Not wanting my hopes to get too high, only to crash and burn later, my weekend goal was to get my business cards out to the public. My plan was to get my name out into the community as a tarot reader. If someone signed up for a reading, that would be all the better.

There were seventeen readers with diverse abilities, and many were well known. They had been on the fair-circuit for years. Attendees had quite a selection: a medical intuitive, psychic mediums, tarot readers, an iris (eye) reader, and a palmist. I asked (more like begged) my guides to be with me, and to give me a sign if participating in festivals was something I was supposed to do.

I'd just finished putting the purple tablecloth on my tarot table, when I noticed a large woman thundering up the aisle, wearing a festival badge. She was built like a linebacker for the San Francisco 49ers, arms out, ready to tackle anyone who got in her way. To be friendly I said, "Hello."

She looked at my banner, and then turned to me and grunted. "I bet you don't even use the traditional tarot deck when you give readings. You use some newfangled *New Age* deck," she spat. Then her head snapped forward, as if she'd heard a referee's whistle. It was clear she wasn't interested in any reply.

The British term "gobsmacked" popped into my mind; a perfect description for how I felt. *What had I gotten myself into?* The smile vanished from my face, and I looked to my girlfriend. Andi was there to assist me and lend moral support, I had no idea I would need her so soon. The doors hadn't even opened.

"Really?" Andi said. "The day hasn't begun and one of the exhibitors has major attitude." Her stylish bob swayed, as she shook her head.

The behavior of that vendor put the fear of God in me. I wasn't sure what to expect from my first festival, but that wasn't anywhere on my list. I'd wanted to respond to the woman, and let her know I used the traditional Rider-Waite tarot deck, but the words had remained stuck in my mouth.

Thank goodness other vendors were cheerful and welcoming. Many came up and introduced themselves. I sat at my reading table and said a silent prayer. I asked God to allow me to be of service to those souls who might sit across from me. I glanced at my iPhone, it showed 10:00 a.m. People began to enter the city of booths.

I'd hoped to entice people to my table by doing a drawing for a free reading. The winner would be selected the week after the festival, and the reading would be conducted at my home or by phone. I loved entering drawings and contests myself, and thought others might enjoy it. Bits of paper were stacked so attendees could write their name and email on it. A container stood nearby for their entries. Andi and I encouraged everyone passing by to enter the drawing and to take a business card.

A lady on a mission marched up to my table. "Are you available to give me a reading right now?"

"I sure am. Please sign in, and then come on back." The moment I had both prayed for and dreaded had arrived.

Once she was seated, I introduced myself. We shook hands, and she said her name was Sally. "Have you ever had a reading before?" I asked.

"I've had several." Sally said, as she readjusted herself in the chair. "I'm afraid I might break this." She motioned to the folding chair. She was a large woman, in her fifties, with shoulder length blonde hair. Sally smoothed several strands into place behind her ear.

"The chair is very sturdy." I assured her.

I explained to her that my readings had evolved into, what I liked to call, a soul reading. Her soul would select cards it wanted to discuss. "That's where I'd like to start anyway, if it's okay with you.

We'll have time for you to ask specific questions after the initial read."

She nodded.

I fanned the shuffled deck from left to right, face down in front of Sally. She carefully chose each card, one at a time, and handed them to me. I placed them into a spread, facing me. As I considered each card, a strange thing happened. A column of energy slammed into my body. I physically felt it lock into position. It covered and aligned my top four chakras.

It's believed that we have seven main energy centers, or chakras, that align to the spine. Areas where consciousness meets matter. The top four swirling energy wheels are: the crown chakra, the third eye chakra, the throat chakra and the heart chakra. It appeared that someone determined they needed adjustment.

I refocused on the cards. Their meanings began to take on a subtle change, and this intrigued me. It was as if a computer download was secretly authorized, and I was told, *you will read differently today, and the cards will hold new expressions.*

I glanced up at Sally to see if she had noticed a change in me, but her eyes remained glued to the cards. I joined her in gazing at the spread.

"Sally, the first card I'd like to talk to you about is the Sacrifice card." I turned it to face her. The artwork depicted a dark haired woman wearing a white sleeveless dress, standing in water, with her arms stretched towards the heavens, palms touching. "I feel that you may be a caregiver for a loved one, or you do it professionally. Much of your time is spent doing for others, so you end up on a back-burner as a result. Does this make sense?"

"It makes perfect sense," Sally said. "I'm a nurse and my shifts are long. I haven't been taking care of myself, and I've been eating horribly." She sat forward and rested her chin on her hands. "I keep telling myself I'm going to be a priority, and take care of myself, but the day never comes. I'm so frustrated."

We discussed what issues bothered her the most, and the small things Sally might do to start an energy shift, to assist her in becoming a priority. During readings, it often happened that information would "drop in." I'd feel compelled to discuss certain topics with the sitter. This reading was no different. I shared some tactics that had worked in my own life, and felt small steps were necessary to not overwhelm Sally. We talked about bringing healthier foods into her diet, like once a week introducing one healthier replacement for something unhealthy she ate. She needed to take it slow, so that she could foster a lifestyle change.

I explained the significance of her remaining cards. I finished with her reading, and Sally asked, "Can I go find my boyfriend? I want him to experience a reading."

"Please do."

Sally left my booth and disappeared down one of the aisles.

Andi turned to me and asked, "Where is she going?"

"Sally is going to get her boyfriend and bring him back."

Andi smiled and gave me a thumbs-up.

Ten minutes later, Sally returned with her boyfriend, Bruce. An agonized look carved his face, as though he might be signing up for a colonoscopy instead of a tarot reading. He was big and beefy, and a sleeve of tattoos covered each arm. From his bicep a large skull seemed to wink at me. Bruce had black hair, and looked to be in his late 50s to early 60s. His size was intimidating and dwarfed the folding chair. *This ought to be interesting.*

As Bruce attempted to get comfortable in the chair, I silently hoped Sally wouldn't stay. Sometimes when a loved one listened in, it prohibited the sitter from being open and frank. I looked at Sally. "Bruce and I will be fine, if you want to explore more of the festival."

Sally insisted on staying, so Andi gave up her chair.

"Have you ever had a reading?" I asked, though I knew the answer.

Bruce's arms folded tightly across his chest. He looked away from me, toward the wall. "No," he mumbled. His body language spoke volumes.

I had my work cut out for me. It was obvious that Bruce was doing the reading to placate his girlfriend. The last place he wanted to be was sitting across from me.

I smiled, putting on my game face, and explained how I read. I asked Bruce to pick his cards.

He looked sideways at his girlfriend, and his meaty hand made quick work of selecting his cards. His tattooed arms locked back into place, a wall of protection.

I took in the cards and had to stifle a chuckle. One of the cards he had chosen was Authority. The picture displayed a dark haired man, large and beefy, with arms folded across his chest Bruce's doppelgänger.

The Financial & Material Changes card *demanded* to be discussed first. It showed a woman's hand, with fingers spread. She wore several rings. My interpretation of the card was that there were either issues in the relationship, or the relationship was new. I shared that interpretation with Bruce and he stole a quick glance at Sally. He looked back to me and said, "Yep."

"Yep, to which one?" I asked.

He stared me down and wouldn't say a word. His eyes were so dark they appeared to be black.

I may need to cut this guy loose, I thought. I had read about having to stop a reading, to release the sitter, but I had never had to do it. Bruce might be my first candidate.

Due to the awkward silence following the question about his relationship, I patted the card and said, "I'm going to leave this card for now." I moved onto the Authority card. "I sense with this card that you are a very good dad, involved with your kids, and very protective."

He grunted and included an affirmative nod.

This was painful. Like dental work without Novocain. I'd never tried to read someone so shut down. I was drawn back to the Financial & Material Changes card. "I feel like there is an issue with your relationship. Would you like to share what's going on?"

Bruce bore a hole in me, refusing to speak.

I let frustration get the better of me, and the words flew out of my mouth. "Are you wanting to break up?" Sally's head whipped around. Now it was her turn to bore a hole into Bruce.

"It's not *that* bad."

An uneasy silence followed. I glanced from one to the other. Sally watching Bruce, Bruce staring at the table, unmoving. *Whatever was going on, I hoped the two of them would talk about it later.*

To break the silence, I said, "I'd like to talk about the next card, if I may?" I turned the Hope card toward Bruce. The drawing showed a person with extended cupped hands. Within the hands, a radiating circle of light. Within the pulsing circle was an alien-looking light-being. The card represented spirituality to me. Either the person was very spiritual/religious or there was work to be done to improve that connection. I asked Bruce, "Are you spiritual or religious in nature, or do you feel you need to do some work in that area?"

Bruce raised his hand, and reached under the neck of his shirt. He pulled out a long thick chain that held a hefty silver cross. He proudly displayed it on his chest, "Very religious."

I was somewhat surprised to hear it, but glad also.

One of his cards nagged at me. It was The Authority card, and I felt it held some additional information. "Bruce, I'm coming back to the father figure card, as I feel there's more to it. Is there something going on with your own father?"

He stared down at the Authority card and spoke in a defeated manner. "He is in a nursing home. My dad has dementia and he is not the father I remember."

Finally, I knew why Bruce was sitting across from me. "Bruce, my mother had dementia and I know how difficult and upsetting it can be to watch a loved one with that condition. I'm so sorry."

His guard crumbled. He looked up at me. "I take my Mother to visit my dad, but it's so hard on me. I don't know how to talk to him anymore." Tears slid down his cheeks. "I do it for my mom, but I have a difficult time being at the nursing home. Dad and I were so close, and we did so many things together. Now there is nothing."

My heart ached. I shared with Bruce that my Mother's long term memory had been better than her short, so it helped to talk about things that had happened long ago. I said, "When I went to visit, I talked about wonderful holidays, birthday parties, and vacations from when I was young. Mom could then participate in the conversations. It brought her joy." I suggested he might want to try this with his dad.

A glimmer of a smile touched his face. "Yes, my Father's long-term memory is somewhat better than his short-term. I'm willing to try anything, because I miss talking to him."

The rest of the reading passed with ease. At the conclusion, I gave Bruce a hug, as well as Sally. My heart went out to them. I didn't envy their car ride home. There was still the relationship issue to tackle.

I checked in with Andi. "You are booked solid for the next couple of hours."

"Are you kidding?"

"No," Andi said. She turned the sign-up sheet so I could take a look.

I was over the moon and floored at the same time. I prayed the next reading would be easier.

I said to Andi, "If I'm going to be sitting for the next couple of hours, I need to visit the ladies' room first." I made a quick getaway.

I did many back-to-back, twenty minute readings for customers. I was thrilled to meet so many new people. Every reading was unique, but some stood out more than others. Like the reading with Bruce. To have a big guy cry and express his feelings was something special to witness, and to be a part of.

While I said goodbye to one client, Andi let me know that my last reading of the day would be back in a minute. My throat was sore, so I took a drink from my water bottle. I wasn't used to talking for hours at a time.

"Hi Carla," Andi said.

I turned and introduced myself, and motioned her toward the table, "Have a seat please." Carla was in her mid to late 30s. She had thick long brown hair, the kind of hair one saw on shampoo commercials. While I shuffled the cards, I told her about my soul readings. The cards were arrayed in front of her. She started to reach slender fingers toward a card, then pulled back, as if struck by a ruler.

"I'm super nervous." Carla said. "I've never had a reading before. I walked past your booth about ten times and just felt drawn to you."

"You are not alone. I've had many 'first timers' today. For some reason I'm attracting virgins." We both laughed.

This time, without hesitation, Carla drew her cards. I arranged them into a spread. I reviewed the cards to get an overall feel for them. Each read was different. Sometimes I would sense the person was troubled, or the cards would reveal the person was emotionally in a good place. Other times, I would *feel* that two or three cards were bound together, and would discuss them so. Then again, it might be that all of the selections needed to be discussed one at a time. Most often, one or two cards *spoke* to me, and I knew I had to start the reading with them.

For Carla's read, the first card that grabbed my attention showed a woman with an expression of sorrow, head bowed. I held it up. "The card you pulled speaks to me of a loved one lost, or a relationship ended." I paused. "Do you understand this?"

Carla's eyes grew big, and she shook her head in disbelief. "Yes, that would be the loss of my mom, and I'm divorced from my husband." Carla told me that her mother had passed away several years ago. Not able to cope with the loss of her mother, she had had a nervous breakdown. "I turned to drugs and alcohol, and was messed up for a long time. It cost me my marriage."

Carla took some time and stared down at the table. She raised her head. "I'm proud to say I have 14 months of sobriety, and attend weekly Alcoholics Anonymous (AA) meetings. I'm so thankful I'm living differently."

I gave her a high five. "Way to go," I said. Once again, I knew why someone was sitting across from me. Carla was the second person that day that had been involved in recovery.

"I think you should know that I've been involved with Al-Anon for over 30 years, and it's no coincidence that you are sitting across from me. I'm sure you are aware that Al-Anon is a support group for people who have either friends or family members with drinking problems. When I started, my Al-Anon sponsor required that I read the Big Book of AA, and had me attend open meetings. She wanted me to understand the family disease of alcoholism from all sides. I've also worked The Twelve Steps of recovery many times."

Carla's eyes were wet. "I was drawn to you for a reason."

As I handed her a tissue, we discussed recovery a bit more. I shared some tools that had helped me succeed in recovery. Journaling had been crucial.

I continued the read and felt the other cards were tied together. I sensed that Carla had some additional emotional work to do. One of her cards was Mental Conflict. I felt that she had been mentally beating herself up and she needed to stop and be gentle with herself regarding the past. A specific issue was troubling her. "I know you've made great strides in recovery, but I feel there is still some additional work. I get that you are chastising yourself about something."

Carla nodded. "I've been working on my 9th Step." She gazed out the window. "There are so many people I need to make amends to. My behavior was less than stellar when I was drunk, and I was not the mother I wanted to be." Turning back to me, she spoke in a hushed tone, "My daughter is at the top of my amends list."

"I think living a sober life is one of the greatest ways you can make daily amends to your daughter. I sure wish I had had a sober mother. Speaking from experience, working the 12 Steps is a pathway to healing and it's clear, you are on your way."

A small smile crept onto Carla's face. "I think so, too."

Just as I finished with the last card, the timer beeped. I thanked Carla for getting a reading and reminded her to take one day at a time. As I watched her walk away, I was hurtled back thirty years to my own story of recovery. Another destiny point that would change my course, my trajectory.

5

God, grant me the serenity
To accept the things I cannot change,
Courage to change the things I can,
And wisdom to know the difference.

The Serenity Prayer

In 1986 I was 28 years old, a veteran of two failed marriages, and living with my parents— again. Their alcoholism had worsened and their relationship was in the *shitter*, as my stepdad would say.

Their marriage had always been shaky. There was always an unease lurking below the surface of their relationship. I knew some of the issues, but others I wouldn't fathom until later.

My parents weren't affectionate with one another. Like Halley's comet, it was a rare sighting to see them kiss or embrace. What they did have between them was humor. Unfortunately, depending on the amount of booze consumed, the humor could veer to sarcasm, maiming those in its path. Due to the volatile home environment, I tried to stay gone. Between work and couch surfing at friends, my efforts were successful.

My latest escape took me to Lake Tahoe for a few days. Returning home, I turned my car onto my parents' driveway. The rocks crunched beneath my tires and announced my arrival.

Getting out of my car, I took in the bright summer morning. The nearby creek of my youth flowed low and quiet. I inhaled deeply, steeling myself before going in.

Looking towards the house, a brown stucco facade with a bright yellow door greeted me. My parents had built our home years earlier, and were proud of its contemporary lines. Visitors often marveled at the indoor atrium, aggregate floors, and roof dome that crackled and popped when the sun warmed it. The only windows facing the street were narrow slits positioned on either side of the lemon-colored door. People often commented on the lack of windows on the front of the house. I grew to be grateful for their absence.

The door opened and my brother's tall lanky frame stood in wait.

"You missed all the excitement," Eddy said.

"What did I miss?" I set my suitcase down.

Eddy flicked his head to move auburn bangs out of his eyes. "A battle royale."

My brother told me the tale of Dad's latest drunk driving ticket. We knew them as 502s, but that may have been "police speak." Mom's reaction to Dad's latest screw-up was to check *herself* into a 30 day treatment center for alcoholism, called Starting Place. Eddy said that Mom was *incommunicado* until she finished her detoxification program.

Detoxification program? I couldn't remember a time when my parents didn't drink. The thought of Mom in a detoxification program was unfathomable. Dad's latest ticket must have pushed her over the edge.

I thanked Eddy for the update, grabbed my suitcase, and headed towards my room.

It was strange not having my mother at home. She stood five foot, two inches tall, but was a force of nature. She had the tenacity of Scarlett O'Hara on steroids. I was grateful she was attempting to do something about her drinking; I had wished for it since I was young. I also understood her wanting to disappear for 30 days.

When I was eleven or twelve, Mom drove Dad (my stepdad) to and from work, and did all the driving for a year, due to *that* drunk driving ticket. I could still picture their snarling faces, and the yelling and screaming that took place over the cost of the ticket, and the attorney's fees. Even without his license, Dad still snuck out and drove to bars. Upon his return, Mom begged him to stop taking risks and stay home, but her pleading went unheard and his addiction always won out.

Growing up in an alcoholic home was never dull. When I turned sixteen, I was drafted by my mother to participate in secret missions. She would insist that we had to *de-wheel* Dad. We would drive from bar to bar in search of his vehicle. Once found, Mom would jump out of the running car and I would get behind the wheel. Mom cranked the engine of Dad's car, and we would race for home. On several nights, Dad came out just as Mom got into his car, then all hell broke loose.

Screaming matches were common. An occasional cocktail glass might fly across the room and shatter into fragments when it hit the aggregate floor.

My parents' friends stopped by for happy hour any day of the week. There were dinner parties where meat was so rare it seemed almost on the hoof. (My dad, three sheets to the wind, may have turned off the barbecue a tad too soon.) Partially eaten meals were left scattered about to be discovered the next morning. It was up to me to clean the kitchen, since I had no hangover, and my stomach wouldn't heave at the first sight and smell of the decomposing dinners.

Since I had a strong stomach, it was my job to assist Mom's girlfriends who drank too much and barfed. I held their hair back as they retched into the toilet, and got washcloths to clean them up afterwards. I thought for a time I'd make a good nurse.

At one dinner party, Fred, a family friend, picked up our dog, Beau Beau. Fred was deep into his cups. He hauled up Beau Beau and said, "Oh you sweet boy!" Fred made smooching sounds since he thought he was staring into our dog's cute button nose, when in reality he had grabbed the opposite end. Beau Beau's front paws clawed the air in double-time, trying to escape the madman who was speaking sweetly into his butthole.

And now, adding to the never ending chaos, my mother was gone. Days went by, and then a call came. Mom had made it through detox and she had a request. She asked me to spend the day with her at Starting Place on Thursday. It was a "family" day. *If it was a family day, why was I the only member being asked to attend?* I had no way of knowing, but my education in recovery was about to begin.

I supported my mother by going to all of the family days during her tenure. Lecture topics included: the family disease of alcoholism, the Big Book of AA, AA meetings for alcoholics, Al-Anon meetings for family and friends, and the 12 Steps of Recovery. A bonus offered to family by Starting Place was free counseling. To receive it, the individual had to attend three Al-Anon meetings and write a paper about their experience. The free counseling seemed a necessity since my second marriage had imploded. I had no clue about how to do relationships.

How poetic to attend my first Al-Anon meeting at the same church where I had married husband number one. *There were no coincidences.* I walked into the room, head down. I felt like I wore the scarlet letter "A" for Alcoholism. I found a chair in the back of the room and dissolved into it. The shock of the evening was the manner in which each person spoke. They were gut-wrenchingly honest. People being forthright was a breath of fresh air. I was drawn in, and like melting candle wax, my walls slid down. I was able to hear and absorb what was being said. Several individuals talked about their alcoholic situations and their own unhealthy behaviors. What a novel concept, that I may have a hand in my own misdeeds. I was familiar with blaming others, but not of owning my own behavior. Some spoke about the measures they'd taken to get healthy. I felt a sense of belonging, safety, and peace, which was strange and new to me. I couldn't wait to attend another meeting, and a glimmer of hope sparked.

Prior to attending that first meeting, I had expected to chalk up the evening to an error in judgement. I'd felt destined to remain on my miserable path of self-loathing. Feeling the shame of two failed marriages. If I'd never gone to that meeting, what would my life have looked like? How much more drinking would I have done? Would I have crossed the line and become an alcoholic like my parents?

Until that night, I'd been in serious training to become the next generation who wore the mantle of "alcoholic." At 28, I was no where near the life I had dreamt. I was not happily married with children, nor having a wonderful career. I was alone, miserable, and living with my parents in my teenage bedroom. I was broken and needed help.

My mother completed the treatment program and didn't drink for a time, but she eventually rejoined Dad in their favorite pastime. I will always be grateful to my mother for being the catalyst that launched me into a clean and sober lifestyle.

I had two things going for me when I started my Al-Anon journey, willingness and clarity. I was willing to do whatever was suggested to get healthy, and it was clear my life didn't work. Having admitted this, I dove into recovery like an Olympian off a high dive. I attended countless meetings and soaked up the presented information. I always had a place to go as meetings were held every night of the week. While living with my parents, Al-Anon became a sanctuary, my 60-90 minutes of sanity.

I gained healthy tools that allowed me to deal with and avoid drama. I read the Al-Anon literature, and learned to keep the focus on myself: I was the only person I had the power to change. It was interesting to see how each family member played a dysfunctional role in the family disease of alcoholism.

One tool I used frequently was the Serenity Prayer. I repeated it like a mantra in difficult situations, to get the focus back on myself.

Getting a sponsor and working the 12 Steps was suggested by members. A sponsor was someone who had a year or more of recovery, and had worked the steps themselves. I chose a woman who attended Adult Children of Alcoholics (ACA), Al-Anon, and AA meetings. Dottie was immersed in recovery. She encouraged me to attend the various meetings, so I could get a well-rounded education on the family disease of alcoholism. Dottie guided me in healthy ways, and was patient. She helped me when I worked through the 12 Steps of Recovery. I still carry her lessons with me.

Spirituality was my primary gift from Al-Anon. I discovered that the happiest and healthiest people in recovery seemed to believe in a higher power. Which higher power didn't seem to matter. It might be God, Source, Jesus, Buddha or Universe, but they all believed in something. I had nothing. I wanted to be the healthiest I could be, so I developed a relationship with a higher power. I explored various churches, but didn't find comfort or a sense of belonging. What resonated, and where I'd felt a sacred presence, was in nature. (Growing up next to a creek might have had a hand in that.)

In the beginning, I prayed to Nature or the Universe. Then over time, I just said God. It was short, easy, and sweet. I looked at God as "Source," or the creative energy of the universe. My goal was to talk to God everyday. I had to have a visual cue to remind me to reach out, or I'd forget. So during my daily commute, a Fresno freeway sign became my cue. When I drove under it, I said, "Hey God, it's Erin." Thus began my talks with God. As time passed, my connection increased and I didn't need the road sign. Praying and chatting to God just came naturally. I wasn't alone anymore. I had a higher power to help me heal and deal with life, and to whom I could turn in times of trouble.

When I first came to Al-Anon there was one saying that haunted me. *You are as sick as your secrets.* Oh boy, I felt like one sick puppy. "Don't tell," was a common phrase drilled into my head, along with, "What would the neighbors think?" I'd been trained to collect secrets like some people amassed baseball cards.

One night at a meeting, a courageous young woman shared her story. She spoke of being sexually molested as a child. I was stunned she said it out loud, to a room full of strangers. I flushed with embarrassment, but I admired her guts.

Not long after, I was asked to chair a meeting, something I'd never done. I was supposed to talk briefly about what my life had been like, how I had come to Al-Anon, and ways my life had improved since. The night I chaired the meeting, I was so nervous I had to sit on my hands to keep them from shaking. I told of being raised in an alcoholic home, including being sexually molested as a child. Releasing my burden and shame brought me to tears. When the meeting was over, people came up to me. They were kind, supportive and thanked me for my honesty. Telling my secret allowed me to physically release it from my body. In an instant, I weighed less.

With the help of God, recovery, my sponsor, and my therapist, I was able to unload many of my character defects. I wrote letters to my mom and Dad to release my frustration, anger, and hurt from being molested, and having my childhood taken from me. I never mailed those letters, I burned them. My parents would never have understood.

After a year in Al-Anon, I was asked by others to be their sponsor. I was honored, and learned more from my sponsees, than I'm sure I ever taught. I continued to be a sponsor for years, and met many brave women and men along the way.

During my recovery, I made new friends who didn't drink. We met at coffee houses, and I noticed how much better I felt not drinking alcohol. I let go of friends who were heavy into drinking. Early on, I made the decision to stop drinking myself. It was far easier to do than I ever imagined. I had a sense that it was up to me to break the cycle, to be the one person from our family who didn't drink. My parents had a difficult time with my decision. They offered me booze at every opportunity. How could a daughter of theirs not drink? I became the black sheep of our family.

While getting healthier, I came up with a plan to set aside as much money as possible. I could do this because my parents' had allowed me to live with them rent free. Within ten months, I'd saved enough for closing costs, and bought myself a one bedroom, 800 square foot home. I glowed with pride as I showed my quaint little place to friends. The tiny bathroom, off to the side of the master bedroom, boasted a clawfoot tub. My new home suited me, and it became a haven.

As my faith and self-esteem grew, I took better care of myself physically and emotionally.

Not drinking alcohol was easy compared to the challenge of not smoking. At the age of twelve, I had taken my first puff while at the creek. I quit on a Monday morning, and then every few seconds I heard in my head, *have a cigarette.* It became a relentless chant that filled my waking thoughts for weeks. To squelch the oral fixation, I loaded up on sugarless candies. I tossed them into my mouth like popcorn. Over time, the demand for a cigarette came less often, thank God. Each time my brain screamed for a cigarette, I responded with, "No, I'm a non-smoker." Quitting smoking took endless resolve, and I'm proud to say that I've been smoke-free for over 30 years.

During recovery, I began to notice how often I used the word "coincidence." The positive things that came my way seemed to come by way of a "coincidence," like how I obtained jobs. I would run into someone I hadn't seen for a time who would mention a job opening. It took awhile for me to grasp, but I believed there were no such things as coincidences. It was my higher power, spirit guides, angels, and loved ones at work. It appeared that once I got on a path that jibed with my soul, I was *led* in a healthy direction.

I've now had over a 30 year relationship with a God of my understanding, and I've had to rely on that higher power many times. I'm never alone unless I choose to be. I now know that I am enough.

I had no inkling that by venturing through the doors of that first Al-Anon meeting, I would be grabbing another destiny point. A point that would change the trajectory of my life and introduce me to the people I would hold most precious: my husband, my step-kids, and my daughter.

6

Betty's Reading

The positive experience at my first festival gave me the confidence to tackle two more endeavors. The first was to explore a new ability, psychometry, and the second was to find more events.

Psychometry is the ability to hold an inanimate object and receive messages or images regarding the person or events related to the object. My favorite astrology book had encouraged Pisces to attempt psychometry, but I had ignored the suggestion for one simple reason: fear of failing. It was difficult to picture myself with a stranger, eyes closed and quiet, while holding an item of theirs. I would look silly. *What if nothing came through, what then?*

I needed to try psychometry in a safe place, and with someone who understood it. I found a four hour class where psychometry was part of the curriculum, taught by a local psychic medium.

During my one-on-one class, the medium selected four of her personal items for me to hold. She handed me a necklace. I cradled it in my palm. The wood beads weighed next to nothing. At the center drape of the necklace hung a small piece of wood etched with oriental writing.

I closed my eyes, breathed deeply, and tried to relax. After a few moments, images and words popped into my head. I wrote down: *Mt. Fuji, live long and prosper, joyful,* and *little boy.* I read my random list to the medium. An odd look swept across her face. The medium said, "I teach classes in Japan."

"You do?"

"Yes," she said. "I had a vision that told me I needed to place a Mt. Shasta crystal on Mt. Fujiyama. So while in Japan, I hired a guide to drive me and some friends to the mountain. The guide deliberated about whether to take us or not, as she didn't want to leave her *little boy* at home. With a great deal of coaxing, the guide agreed and took us to several sacred places along *Mt. Fuji.* I was *joyful* because my vision became a reality. The crystal that had traveled with me was left on Mt. Fuji. At one stop, I bought 'safe travel' necklaces for my companions, but for myself, I purchased the *'prosperity'* necklace. That is the one your are holding. So the information you received, makes sense." She told me her students didn't usually come up with such specific details during a class.

I was amazed because the information had floated in easily. I held three additional objects and had "hits" on those as well. After completing that portion of the class, I felt encouraged and somewhat spooked.

I knew to develop an ability I had to practice it, so I needed another safe environment. I planned to ask several acquaintances who were into this kind of stuff to come over and bring three items. I didn't want close friends, because I didn't want information received to be tainted by what I already knew about them. I explained to my "volunteers" that I was trying to develop an ability, and I needed to get comfortable with the process. I asked them to bring objects of their own, or from loved ones who had passed.

I had several dates scheduled, and asked for guidance from Spirit. The evenings I practiced psychometry were fun and enlightening. Since I didn't know much about the gals who were assisting me, it made the "hits" on the objects that much more powerful and surreal.

One friend, Sonia, brought her goodies in a decorative bag. Holding the first two items went well. The last item was a black box. She lifted the lid to reveal a pale-pink crystal lotus flower. The flower was four inches in diameter, and each petal was an individual crystal. Several of the petals were broken; it was too delicate to hold. Nestled next to the flower lay a single chandelier crystal. I picked it up with care. I took a deep breath and closed my eyes. Images and feelings began presenting themselves.

The first sensation I felt was an energy. The energy of a *grandmother,* or a *matronly woman* came through. Spirit showed me the top of her head, and I saw a *bouffant hairdo* with *brownish/auburn hair.* The time period felt like the 1960s. The spirit wore a stylish skirt and jacket, and I got the impression the woman had been *fashion conscious,* unlike me. Next I saw a *basket full of eggs.* It seemed the image might have two interpretations. The basket could have been used to go to a rural market of long ago, to collect eggs, or it could be a message for Sonia to *not put all her eggs in one basket* regarding work. She needed to diversify.

Sonia, a petite blonde in her early forties, looked quite happy after I read my list to her and described the feelings associated with each item.

She said, "The crystal and flower belonged to my former roommate who was older, and Frances did have a grandmother energy. She was such a lovely woman and passed a few years ago." Sonia paused to collect herself, and then continued. "She grew up in London, and very well could have used a *basket* to collect eggs, but I don't know that for sure. As a young adult she became a nurse and married a doctor. They moved to the United States when they were young. Frances was very *fashionable* and clothes were important to her. I have pictures of her wearing her *brownish/auburn hair* in a *bouffant* style." Sonia reached for her cell phone and scrolled through photos until she found the one she wanted. She turned the phone toward me and pointed out a woman with teased hair wearing a nice suit. It appeared to be a family portrait taken in the 1960s.

"Oh how wonderful," I said. I was gratified to see that the picture of Frances matched the image I'd been given. I thanked Sonia for her help with the psychometry exercises. Working with "volunteers," and out of my home, had enabled me to feel safe. Feeling comfortable had been a key component in the positive results.

Encouraged by the practice runs, I decided to offer psychometry at the end of my tarot readings. I would not charge for holding objects, since it was a developing ability. I would inform clients that I was practicing a new skill, and see if they were interested in helping by allowing me to hold something of theirs.

My second endeavor was to find other events where I could do tarot readings. I visited new friends I'd made at the Healing Arts Festival. Sherri and Sheri ran a business called Wings Over Soul. I affectionately called them the Sherris. They were kind and helpful, and shared what it had taken to get their business off the ground. They sold rocks, gems, crystals, jewelry, and medicine bags. They traveled most weekends to various fairs. I asked if they could suggest some venues. They recommended several, and one was only a couple of months away. It was a festival held in Reno, and I took quick action and bought a space.

The Reno Convention Center was the venue, and I booked a room across the street at the Atlantis Casino Resort Spa. I'm not well-traveled, so having the two buildings in close proximity made me feel better. I was also grateful that Prasanna agreed to go with me and would be my moral support and assistant.

Due to expense, I purchased a smaller booth, an 8' X 8'. Since I didn't sell product, it was always harder to cover the cost of a booth doing readings only. I readied my spot, and the privacy screens added a zen-like quality to my space. On top of the stacked tarot cards rested a selenite crystal.

A gemstone known to clear energy, and it worked for my cards.

To the right of my booth stood a six foot banner: *Tarot Readings by Erin*. Below that a hummingbird hovered over a delicate lotus flower. The background was done in pale pinks and purples. Beneath the image of the lotus flower were the words:

At A Crossroads?

Just Curious?

Let's Explore!

The banner was striking and drew many people.

I said prayers for protection and guidance, and set my intentions for the day.

Since this was my first time in Reno, I wasn't sure how busy I'd be. It didn't take long to find out. Prasanna had people who wanted a reading to add their name on my sign-up sheet. I had just finished one customer, when a young woman walked up to my booth. She had short black hair and wore black glasses. Betty seemed young, maybe in her early 20s. She asked about my tarot readings. I explained how I worked, and how I started with a soul reading. Betty pushed her glasses back to the bridge of her nose and said, "I'd like to get a reading." She told me she returned to this psychic fair every year to get a reading from one specific reader.

Each visit she also got a reading from someone new, and I was that someone new.

Betty had come prepared. She pulled a hand-held recording device from her purse, and asked if it was okay to record. I agreed. I shuffled the tarot cards and fanned them before her. Betty ran her hand above the cards as if checking for heat. She selected her cards and passed them to me, one at a time. As I turned them over, I placed them into a "Tell Me A Story" spread. The first card was in the center, the other four cards were at the corners of the center card, starting at the top left position.

The first card that spoke to me was The Hanging Man. It showed a colorfully clad gentleman suspended upside-down, held by a gold chain around his ankle. He appeared to not have a care in the world. I turned the card towards Betty. "When this card is drawn, it tells me of a situation or person you need to release. Or you need a different perspective on the matter or person. What is it you need to let go of?"

She kept her eyes downcast and answered, "My childhood."

Data comes to me in various forms during a reading. Receiving images on my internal screen, between my eyebrows, is called Clairvoyance, or "clear seeing." When I hear a word, name, or a phrase, that is known as Clairaudience, or "clear hearing." Sometimes, I just "know" something, and that is called Claircognizance. When I "feel" something, that is known as Clairsentience. The best way to describe my internal experience is to say information just drops into my awareness.

When Betty said that her childhood was what she needed to let go of, I *knew* she had been sexually molested as a child. Molestation was a delicate issue, and yet I had to trust and honor the information I received intuitively. That's how my intuition developed. I said, "There is no easy way to ask this, so I'm going to be direct. Were you sexually molested as a child?"

Her eyes flew open. She replied in a hushed voice, "Yes."

"That's the reason you are sitting across from me, that's why you're here. I was also sexually molested as a child. Spirit brought us together for a purpose."

Betty attempted to hold back tears, but was not successful. I passed a Kleenex box to her. I learned she had recently started to tackle her emotions about being molested. I shared some of the tools that had helped me heal and forgive. Counseling, journaling, and taking care of oneself, were a few of the tools discussed. "Have you ever done any journaling?"

She shook her head no. "I'm ready to try anything at this point."

"I have found it helpful over the years," I said. "Writing is a way I can get something physically out of my head and onto paper. It's not only a physical release, but an emotional one as well."

The next card I turned toward her represented a male authority figure, The Emperor. "I believe this card is tied to you being sexually molested. It feels like a family member or a friend of the family may have been responsible. Does this make sense?"

Tears streamed down her face. Betty nodded. "It was my dad. The abuse went on for years. Our home life was so crazy. My mom finally left him and I testified against him when I was twelve. He's been locked up for years in a psychiatric ward, due to the physical and emotional abuse he inflicted on us."

"I'm so sorry." It pained me to learn of another casualty of abuse, and to hear of another childhood stolen. Again, I encouraged Betty to seek professional help, and explained some therapists might work on a sliding scale, if money was an issue.

"I haven't had any counseling since I was twelve," Betty said, wiping away a tear. "I know I need to go back and let go of the hurt. I didn't realize how the past was still affecting my present."

The rest of her cards encouraged her to speak her truth and to continue to have hope. Betty's reading had been so emotional, I had to ask, "Do you still want to try psychometry?"

She brightened. "I've never experienced it before, so I would like to try it." She grabbed a plastic green four-leaf clover key-chain from her purse. "Can you hold this?"

"Sure," I said, as I reached for my pad of paper and pen. I held the key-chain and closed my eyes. I focussed on my internal screen, and asked my guides for assistance. The images can be past, present, or future, so it's not uncommon for some items to go unidentified, as they might be future. Sometimes the images don't make sense until later, and other times what I receive could be incorrect. This intuitive stuff wasn't a science, and I was definitely a work in progress, but whatever spirit gave me, I documented.

I said to Betty, "I know I'm holding a four-leaf clover, but the first thing I heard was *Erin Go Bragh* and *grandma*. I feel a grandmother energy coming through." (Erin Go Bragh was a phrase I'd heard my entire life, since my name is Erin. I was told it meant "Ireland Forever.") I asked Betty, "Do you have a grandmother who passed, and was she Irish?"

Betty smiled. "Yes, my grandmother was Irish." She told me how close they had been, and that her grandmother had passed a few years ago. "I always feel her presence."

"She's with us now." I said.

I went on to the next item. "I saw a polished wooden *ladder* in a large, wood-paneled library, like you see in old movies. It's a ladder that can slide across a wall to access books. Does this mean anything to you?"

Betty laughed. "I used to work at a library and had to go up and down a ladder like that, all day long. I know exactly what you are seeing."

"The next image given was of an *antique cash register*. It was made of silver and had ornate carvings of leaves and flowers carved on the body. It had black manual push-keys with the dollars and cents marked on top."

"Wow." Betty said. "I just quit the library and opened my own business. My store is full of antiques, and I do have an antique cash register."

"Congratulations on your new business!" I said. We discussed the rest of the list and a few items didn't resonate with her, so they might have been related to the future. When our time was up, she turned off her recorder.

Betty said, "I sure didn't expect to discuss my childhood today, but I guess I needed to. Thanks for the reading. It was both helpful, and fun."

While she walked away, I said a silent prayer for healing. I knew she had a lot of work ahead of her. Talking to Betty took me back to my own story of abuse, and how I'd survived and eventually thrived.

The First Destiny Point

etty, from the Reno psychic fair, was not the first woman to sit across from me who had been sexually molested. They never came to discuss being violated, but the soul read opened the door to their hidden grief.

I believed these women and I shared similar frequencies or vibrations. People often told me they had been "drawn" to me, and I *knew* it happened for our mutual growth. Betty said she had needed to let go of her childhood. I, too, had had to let go, so I wouldn't be held prisoner to past events.

The first ten years of my life were wonderful and carefree. I lived with my grandmother, JoJo. The story went I couldn't pronounce Josephine so I called her JoJo. *Why not just call her Grandma or Nana?* That story was never revealed to me.

Mother and I lived with my grandparents because she had divorced my biological father when I was one. (I didn't meet my father until I was twenty years old, and that's a tale for another time.) Mom gave birth to me at twenty-one. My origin was the unexpected result of fooling around while dating.

My grandparents adored me, but especially my grandfather, Little Daddy. JoJo delighted in talking about him, and his Scottish heritage. There were tales of kilts and bagpipes, and ancestors from the Isle of Skye.

I heard marvelous stories of how Little Daddy let me ride his shoulders as he paraded me around town. We were buddies. Pictures and a few sweet memories are all that I have left of him. He passed away when I was four. My mother later confided that his passing was the worst thing that had ever happened to her.

One treasured memory is of Little Daddy and me playing hide and seek. I lay on my twin bed hidden under the sheets, invisible to the outside world. Or so I thought. I heard my grandfather whisper, "Where's Erin? Where could she be?" Giggling, I threw back the sheets. "Here I am." Little Daddy gasped, hands went to each of his cheeks, a look of utter shock etched his face. My mother watched from her make-up table, in on the fun.

Our home was located on an acre of land next to a creek. When the weeds grew tall, I trudged through them creating a corridor down to the water. That creek became a place of enchantment. The sights and sounds of the landscape held magic, and I spent endless hours there; it was a time of innocence.

My first ten years on the planet fell between 1958 to 1968. Kids played outside from sun-up to sundown. Parents yelled for them to come home for dinner, or to come in for the evening.

Being a tomboy and loving sports made it easy to be with boys. I enjoyed them, still do. Many of the kids, mostly boys, would meet up to play hide and seek, touch football, ride bikes, or hang out at the creek. That waterway offered unlimited entertainment due to the various animals and bugs that called it home. I waded into the water, up to my thighs, to catch minnows, tadpoles, guppies, toads and bullfrogs. Large tadpoles were my favorite because they reminded me of a big toe with a tail. I cut my feet a few times on broken glass hidden in the muddy bottom, but that didn't stop me from venturing back in. (Once, when I cut my foot, Dad heard my cries and raced to the creek. He bent to look at the blood gushing from the gash, and I saw terror fill his face. His expression made me bawl even louder. With a sudden jerk, he picked me up and ran me home for doctoring.)

A beautiful weeping willow stood at the creek, near my grandparents' property. One huge branch bent towards the ground like an elephant's trunk. Kids could scoot down it like a slide, or we could straddle it like a horse. It became anything we imagined. Grasping the green smaller branches of the tree, we became Tarzan and let out a yell as we swung back and forth across the creek. The spot kept me spellbound for many years.

When I was five years old, an odd thing happened. Mom moved out of JoJo's house and I had our bedroom all to myself. She moved to a duplex with her new husband, my stepdad, and lickety-split, I had a new baby brother.

After watching a Perry Como Christmas Special on TV, it dawned on me that my dad looked similar to Mr. Como, and I said so. They were both attractive, and each wore a hairstyle cropped close to their head. At six foot, Dad stood a good six inches taller than the singer. I noticed Mr. Como didn't swear once on his show, but Dad knew a lot of cuss words and threw them around like confetti. Another difference: I never heard Dad sing.

When my parents came to visit, I saw my brother for the first time. I heard my name vibrating across the cool spring air, my mom calling me home. I ran from the creek to the back of the house, and stood in front of the big picture window. Mom sat on the couch and held a small bundle. I cupped my hand to the glass and peered in. I watched as his small face screwed up, as if he'd just been pinched. Far too small to come to the creek and play, and of no use to me. I waved to everyone and headed back to my friends.

I loved JoJo with all my heart. A substantial woman, my grandmother, who ruled from a green overstuffed chair, her throne. She dyed her grey hair black, but not often enough, since it stayed two-toned much of the time. JoJo wore tropical-colored *muumuus*. That word made me laugh. How could a muumuu be a dress when everyone knew it was the sound a cow made?

Tiered tables hugged the side of JoJo's royal seat. They held a rotary phone, empty glasses, discarded clip-on earrings, and pill bottles that I was warned never to touch. One pill bottle contained little red candies, or so I thought. I was tempted. JoJo said the red pills helped her sleep.

My grandmother didn't walk much and rarely left the house. She used what little energy she had to scoot a walker to the kitchen to make herself a drink. JoJo swore the whiskey was for medicinal purposes, to help clear the phlegm from her throat. I made the mistake of asking her about phlegm, and her explanation grossed me out. When JoJo wasn't looking, I snuck a sip of whiskey. The taste made me gag and it burned my tongue. I was so happy my throat wasn't riddled with phlegm.

My mom looked like the old Dean Martin song, *five foot two, eyes of blue.* She had short teased blonde hair with enough hairspray to hold it firm in a wind tunnel. Standing weekly appointments at the beauty parlor were necessary to keep her look pristine. Her obsession to protect her hair between appointments prevented her from living life to the fullest. No swimming or getting her hair wet. That was too high a price for beauty. I pledged to always manage my own hair.

Mom's attention to her looks paid off. I thought her beautiful and so did others. My curse was that I didn't look anything like her. I had long brown frizzy-wavy hair that had a mind of its own. My almond-shaped hazel eyes disappeared when I smiled, hinting at some unknown Asian ancestor. I dreamt of being small, blue-eyed and blonde, but I never woke up that way. No one ever used the word petite to describe me. Boys called me and a girlfriend Amazon Women after we had studied them in school. I was proud to be thought of as a female warrior.

My mother swung by JoJo's after she taught school to make sure we were okay and had food. Mom began each visit with the same greeting.

"Hi, how is JoJo doing? How much did she drink today?" Mother called at times, and requested I secretly mark the Sunny Brook bottle so she would know how much JoJo had had to drink. I marked bottles with a crayon. (I was being trained to be an enabler at the age of five. I learned how to keep secrets and to focus on others. I knew more about another person than I did of myself.)

After Mom saw to our needs, she would kiss me goodbye and make her way to the "duplex." I stayed the night there from time-to-time, and saw my little brother, Eddy, but I had to go back to JoJo's. She gave my Mother grief for my absences.

On Saturdays, Mom and I went to a little market and bought food for both homes. Red, the butcher, always gave me a lollipop, so I enjoyed shopping. I didn't like it when his apron was covered in blood. Mom would drive back to JoJo's house and put away our groceries, and then leave for the duplex. She was one busy lady.

I had a great deal of freedom living with my grandmother. Today it frightens me to look back and think of walking to and from school by myself at five, six and seven. I had the run of the neighborhood, and crossed busy streets to go to the Dime Store. A magical place of candy and toys. JoJo warned me not go by myself, but I snuck anyway. I knew she couldn't do anything about it, since she could barely walk. This time of freedom and independence seeped into my soul. I had no idea this period of grace would save me later.

For over two years, it was JoJo and I. During that time her drinking increased and she took many falls. I called my parents and they would make a special trip so Dad could pick JoJo off the floor and get her back into her green chair. A fight would follow about her drinking, falling, and bathroom accidents.

One horrible day I discovered JoJo on the carpet, sitting in a pool of diarrhea. It had run down her legs, leaving a snail's trail. I called and called, trying to reach my parents, but the phone just continued to ring.

"Please help me up," JoJo wailed.

"No, I'm not big enough." I said. We repeated this conversation many times.

I cleaned JoJo up the best I could, but my efforts took on the appearance of a finger-painting exercise gone wrong. The smell of my artwork overpowered my nose and drove me backwards.

JoJo kept begging me to pick her up. I wanted to help her, but she was too heavy and drunk. At one point, I hid down the hallway, covering my ears, hoping her whining would stop. Dad had made me promise to never try to pick her up. He said I would get hurt.

She continued to holler my name, and it became like an episode from the Twilight Zone. When I couldn't take her screeching any longer, I stomped down the hallway and yelled, "Stop calling my name!" She begged in a half-cry, as only a drunk can. My jaw clenched, and I hauled her ass up off the floor. She made a mad grab for her walker, and somehow remained standing.

Later, I reached my parents and told them of the day's events. Mom and Dad raced over. They never understood how JoJo had made it to the kitchen for drinks, but not to the bathroom. Not long after this incident, my parents and brother moved in.

I loved having my family under one roof. My brother, Eddy, moved into my room, and took over the other twin bed. My parents claimed a tiny bedroom the size of a closet. It had a double bed and one dresser. Dad's size twelve feet dangled over the bottom of the mattress. When the door stood wide open it hit the foot of the bed. I don't know how they managed it. When Eddy or I climbed into their bed to visit, it was like the last fish being squeezed into a sardine tin.

A favorite family memory is of my mom, Dad, Eddy and me, lying in the backyard to escape the heat of the house. The window-mounted air-conditioner was no match for the relentless Sacramento hot-spells. To feel any relief one had to stand in front of the unit. I did this with arms spread like an eagle, talking into the air-conditioner so I could listen to my distorted voice. I was easily entertained as a child.

When the temperature outside became lower than the temperature inside, we fled the house. We would lie on a large bedspread on the lawn and let the cool Delta breeze wash over us. When the stars appeared, our parents pointed out the North Star and the Big Dipper, and told us what they knew of the constellation. The bullfrogs sang us to sleep.

Mom knew what do in a kitchen. She made delicious meals and we ate together at the kitchen table, or out on the back patio. Our dogs circled under the picnic table, waiting for tidbits of food my brother and I didn't like. JoJo never joined us, she ate in her chair. Cocktail hour was every night at five o'clock. The start time got earlier as the years went on.

From ages eight to eleven, I witnessed the progression of my grandmother's and parents' alcoholism. My dad found it necessary to stop at local bars before he came home. I felt my Mother's tension as she glanced from the clock to the driveway, waiting for his arrival. Dad came in late, and was met by Mom's fury. She wanted him to come straight home from work, and not spend family money in the bars. In the early days, it was one day out of the work week, but in the end, it was daily. Dad frequented bars as regularly as the daily newspaper was tossed onto our front porch. Mom asked him why he just couldn't come home to his family. But she eventually gave up. Her address book was filled with the phone numbers of his favorite watering holes. Later, the same address book helped me locate my parents, so I could ask permission to spend the night at a friend's.

JoJo found her own sneaky ways to obtain more booze since my parents were allotting her two drinks per night. Mom discovered half-consumed bottles of whiskey in JoJo's dresser and closet.

Mom would stand before JoJo, arm extended with Exhibit A in hand. "What's this?"

JoJo hung her head, lips zipped tight; she refused to speak.

We learned that my grandmother had paid taxi drivers to buy the alcohol, and deliver it to her while we were away. She also bribed the cleaning lady to bring her whiskey. She gave new meaning to "where there's a will, there's a way."

When I was eleven, on a night like any other, my brother and I kissed my parents and JoJo goodnight. We went to our room, climbed into our separate beds, and fell asleep. But unlike other nights, someone else was in our room. I became aware that Dad was rubbing my back. Exhausted from a full day of play, I wanted to slip back into my comatose state. I didn't move or acknowledge him. I had almost returned to sleep when his hand crept from my back and slid under my nightie. His hand traveled under my panties, finding what he searched. Fingernails sliced into sensitive tissue.

Filled with pain, terror, and confusion, I held my breath and froze. I inwardly begged him to stop touching me *there*. *Please stop, please stop, it hurts* repeated over and over in my head. I don't know how long he remained in the room, but it seemed like forever.

Once he stopped touching me, he adjusted my clothes, covered me, patted my back, and left. My mind raced. I wracked my brain trying to figure out what I could have said or done to make Dad hurt me so. I knew his coming into my room wasn't right. Why would he do this? *Where was Mom?* I had no answers.

It was 1969. There were only three television stations and no World Wide Web. No forum existed where alcoholism and molestation were openly discussed.

There were no commercials or school programs that taught children about their bodies, or that their private parts were off limits to others. There was no guidance on whom to contact if you had been a victim of sexual abuse. At eleven, I wasn't equipped to deal with my situation, and struggled to make sense of it. I felt so alone.

I now had a horrible secret that weighed on me, making it difficult to breath. I didn't know if or how to talk to my mother about it.

The next day my dad treated me as if nothing had happened, which confused me even more. Still sore, I knew I hadn't dreamt the event. I convinced myself that it must have been some kind of accident, and that it would never happen again. It was a young girl's wish, but it was not to be.

I can't remember the exact number of times Dad invaded my bedroom to violate me, but his pattern remained the same. He'd wait until everyone was asleep. Once I felt his presence, fear paralyzed me. I prayed my mom would save me, but that never happened. It became clear that if I didn't do something, it would never stop. I was afraid of my dad now, and I wanted the old one back. The one I'd enjoyed and felt comfortable with. The solution was to tell my Mother. She could get him to stop.

How should I start the conversation? I understood secrets, and knew I must wait until my Mother and I were alone. When that happened, I gathered up all of my eleven year old courage and began. When I explained where Dad had touched me, Mom looked as if I were speaking a foreign language. Her blank stare made it obvious that her brain wasn't grasping what I had told her. She said, "You must be mistaken. I'm sure he didn't touch you there."

"I'm not lying."

It had never occurred to me that my mom wouldn't believe me, and that frightened me even more. Angry and incredulous, her face flushed. I tried to convince her I was telling the truth.

Suddenly, her body sagged, like the air escaping a balloon. She raised her head and stared out the window. When she spoke, she sounded defeated. "I'll talk to him . . . and it will stop."

"Thank you." I said, and threw my arms around her neck. Her arms remained at her sides.

That evening a huge fight erupted between my parents. They yelled and screamed, and I could hear my name. Lying in bed, I clenched the sheets in fear. I couldn't believe my brother slept. I wanted the fighting to stop, which it eventually did. Days of uneasy silence followed. Walking through the house was like walking through a mine field, one wrong step might detonate another explosion.

Confiding in my mother brought the desired outcome. Dad never touched me again. Mom had protected me. I believed life would return to the way it had been. But it never did.

I was too young to understand that telling my secret, would cost me both parents. Trusting Dad was impossible. I didn't want to be alone with him, especially after he'd been drinking. I felt safer when a third person was in the room with us. To add to my discomfort, my Mother's attitude toward me changed. I had gone from being a daughter to "the other woman."

At times, when Mom found Dad and me in conversation, she would say hurtful things. She'd storm into the room and yell, "You can talk to *her,* but you can't talk to me." I didn't know how to deal with her. I tried to put her at ease and tell her our talking was nothing. The entire situation seemed bizarre, and I didn't understand the change that had taken place in our home. My parents still provided for me, but gone were the trust, closeness and innocence I had once known.

Back in 1969 we looked like a normal family on the outside, but on the inside it was a different story. Our family secret festered over the years. When my parents were drunk, they hurled hurtful remarks about my dating. They called me a whore and a slut, even though I was still a virgin. These attacks shattered my self-esteem, and the effects took years to fully heal.

Telling my mother about being molested was my *first* destiny point, the first fork on my road. I believe we all have them, events that shift us from one path to another. I've thought long and hard about this destiny point. What if I had kept my secret and not told my mother? How many more years of sexual abuse would have followed? What kind of person would I have become? Telling my mother was part of my soul journey, and part of my soul's evolution. I wanted to protect myself, and that led to a course change. I learned to become my own parent.

Years later, in Al-Anon, I discovered that sexual abuse was common in alcoholic homes. Being sexually molested allowed me to understand and relate to women in recovery. Talking to those women and my counselors enabled me to heal, grow, and forgive. Eventually, during tarot card readings, I had opportunities to share my hope and strength with women who had suffered similar experiences. I know now it was what I was meant to do.

The Teen Years

On one level my teen years were normal. I experienced happy and peaceful times: barbecues, swimming and boating on Folsom Lake. I went to school, did homework, babysat, and did chores.

On another level, it was bizarre and painful. I would wake at 3:00 a.m. to screaming: my parents fighting again. Sometimes I tried to be their referee, but mostly I stayed huddled in my bed, praying for the storm to pass.

I dreaded winter: a season of intense arguments and bill collectors' calls. Dad worked for a company that built roads and highways. When the wet weather hit, the work dried up. He could be unemployed for months. Not working gave him far too much time to visit his favorite watering holes.

Mom and I were in the kitchen, and I watched her uncap a black marker and write "D.O." on her calendar. The month of December hung from a nail on the side of a brown cabinet. I couldn't understand why she had so many things to "do."

"What does D.O. stand for?" I asked.

Her brows pressed together and she pursed her lips. It seemed a battle waged on whether she should reveal her cryptic message. She sighed. "It stands for Dad Out. It's when he's out drinking all day or night."

"Oh," was all I dared.

During these times it was my dad's habit, after the bars had closed, to stagger into our house with a new "buddy" who had given him a ride home. Sometimes I slept through their party. At other times, I was well aware of a stranger in our home.

At fifteen, I woke to a man coming into my bedroom. The light from the hallway behind him turned him into a ghostly silhouette. I bolted up. "This isn't the bathroom. It's down the hall."

Instead of retreating, he hit the switch of the overhead light and stepped into the room. I squinted.

His short stature, long arms, and unkempt brown hair gave him an apelike appearance. Bloodshot eyes fixed on me. I panicked and yelled, "Get out of my room."

The man advanced, arms out. "Quiet now, quiet," he whispered.

I jumped up on my bed, in a full granny nightgown, in fight or flight mode. "Get out." I screamed.

My dad appeared behind him, weaving from side-to-side. He grabbed the door frame to steady himself. Mom joined the fray, screeching at the man to get out. I leapt off my bed, ducked under the arms of the stranger, and rushed out of the room. My mother hustled me to the front door.

"Run to Janet's house . . . now!" She pushed me out onto the walkway. The door slammed behind me.

I ran barefoot on the cold pavement, not caring that my feet hurt. The familiar street seemed different in the morning hours. The moonlight created eerie shadows as it seeped through the trees and bushes that lined the road. I heard a branch snap and imagined someone coming after me; fear quickened my gait. Scrambling across Janet's front yard, I pounded my fist on the oak door until someone answered. It was 3:30 a.m. Fear dissolved into shame and embarrassment. I could not meet

Janet's eyes as I explained the chaos I'd just left. She squeezed my shoulder as she let me in.

Sometimes the men who drank with and taxied Dad home were nice. Sometimes they were sketchy, like Springtime; his arms sleeved in tattoos. He'd done time in Folsom Prison, but I never knew why. Dad had him work on our cars because he needed money.

Then there were some men who would leave Dad to follow me across the sunlit atrium, to ask me out. An age difference of twenty-five to thirty years existed, but it didn't deter them. The gulf in ages may have been the attraction.

I learned to expect the unexpected. I waited for the other shoe to drop because I knew it would. And if it didn't drop, it was thrown.

When I was thirteen my mother and I had a serious discussion about JoJo's alcoholism. My mom never wanted to be like her mother, and she made me swear that I would confront her if I believed her drinking had risen to that level. I promised her but never dreamed it could happen. Little did I know how much drinking she would do in the next three years.

I heard retching and gagging. The horrible sounds came from my mother's bathroom. I pictured her in a nightie, on her knees, white-knuckles gripping the toilet seat. I'd seen her crouched like this before. It took everything I had to quiet my own stomach, and not reflex gag. We would not be doing lunch as planned. Another weekend with Mom deathly ill from a hangover. I had to confront her.

I entered the cavelike bedroom. Her small form a lump under the covers. "How are you feeling?"

Dead silence. Inching my way up the side of the kingsize bed, I pulled the chain on the lamp on the nightstand. I eased down on the edge of the bed, trying not to create too much movement. Her matted blonde hair clung to her head like a helmet. The dark circles under her eyes stood out against her grey-tinged face. She stared up at me, lips pressed together.

It was now or never.

"Mom, do you remember when you made me promise to tell you if I thought your drinking had become like JoJo's?"

Her eyes widened. "Yes."

"I think that time has come. This is another weekend when you've been throwing-up from partying the night before. Sometimes you ask me what you and Dad were fighting about because you can't remember. It seems you have to drink every day now, and I'm worried."

My mom pushed up off the mattress, and sat rigid against the walnut headboard. With veins showing on the sides of her neck, she growled, "How can you say that about me? I'm nothing like my mother." Her fury pumped a ruddy color into her cheeks. She stabbed her index finger, nailing my chest. "You have no idea what you are talking about."

I stood up and stepped back, rubbing my chest. "You made me swear, and I'm keeping my promise. I think your drinking is out of control. I've done my part." I turned to leave.

She snarled at my retreating back. "You don't know anything, you're only sixteen. I'm nothing like JoJo."

My trembling hand encircled the knob and I banged the door closed. I sprinted out the front door to escape. The outdoors was a refuge and a place to get my feelings under control. To survive my home, I learned to stuff my hurt and pain down like overflowing trash in a garbage bin. Vulnerability was not a desirable survival trait. I resolved to not let my parents know how much they wounded me. With each altercation, like a strawberry in chocolate, I dipped my heart in concrete. A coping mechanism developed where I'd "shut-down" around my parents. I discovered if I voiced hurt over a remark, more torment ensued. If I remained silent and hid my anguish, life seemed somewhat more tolerable.

One such lesson occurred in junior high. After dinner, Dad and I were in the family room watching TV. He sat on the loveseat with an Old Fashioned in one hand, and a cigarette in the other. I was on the sofa. From the corner of my eye, I saw him take a long pull from his drink. Dad's eyes crinkled as he grinned at me. "I can say one positive thing about you."

I stiffened. "What is that?"

He chuckled. "You don't really sweat much for a fat girl." He thought this hilarious and laughter filled the room.

I was not laughing. My hands moved to conceal my belly. I was sensitive about my weight. It was the era of Hostess Ding Dongs and Ho Hos, and we had a cupboard full. I ate my feelings. When I glanced into a mirror I saw a pudgy unattractive girl with frizzy brown hair, an image not seen in Teen magazines. His joke pierced me. I'd seen Dad clean fish he'd caught; his words gutted me.

"What's wrong? Don't you think that's funny?"

"No, I don't." Tears streamed down my cheeks. I wiped them with my sleeve. "That hurt . . . my feelings."

"Come on . . . can't you take a joke? Where's your sense of humor?"

Choking back tears, I got up from the sofa and retreated into my bedroom. I would suffer the "joke" many times over. Telling Dad he'd hurt my feelings had no impact; so I pledged to keep my emotions to myself. I crawled into bed and embraced my pillow.

I'd always liked boys; I even had a boyfriend in nursery school. There'd always been someone I was interested in, through grade school, junior high, and high school. My liking boys was innocent enough when young; Dad paid no attention to my Prince Charmings. But after Dad sexually abused me, his attitude changed. He took a keen interest in the boys that came around the house, and he didn't like any of them.

To survive, I tucked away the molestations into a secret compartment deep within. I tried never to think of it. I was one of the lucky ones, in the sense that the abuse didn't prevent me from exploring and enjoying my own sexuality with the boys and men I'd come to love. I felt normal in that aspect of my life, especially when I compared my sexual experiences to girlfriends'.

My first high school boyfriend lived up the street. Because he didn't get along with his own parents, he stayed with a lovely Italian family. My dad would not meet him, and forbade me to see him because of our age difference, his eighteen to my fifteen. It put me in a situation of having to lie to my parents, but I couldn't give him up. So I lied and told my parents I was at the movies with girlfriends when I was with Jeff.

There were many fights about not being allowed to see Jeff. When I confronted Dad that I hated having to lie, he relented in a small way. Jeff could park in our driveway, and I could go out and sit in his VW Bug. In winter, we watched as our conversations floated out like smoke and covered the small windshield. To warm us, he'd periodically start the Bug. We had to raise our voices to be heard over the engine noise. It was a ridiculous situation. If my dad hadn't said I couldn't see Jeff, I'm sure the relationship would have fizzled out within a month. As it was, it lasted six months.

I knew Dad had inappropriate feelings for me. He kept them under wraps when sober, but they awoke when he was drunk and we were alone. An alcoholic tends to spend a great deal of time under the influence, so I tried to be away from home as much as possible. School activities and homework helped, but getting a job at fifteen and a half clinched it. I worked at a Jimboy's Tacos restaurant. I loved having a job and my own money. It gave me a bigger picture of the world and confidence in myself. Work provided a new social life and tremendous joy. It was also where I met Frank.

He sauntered into the restaurant, stepped to the counter, and I looked up into light-green eyes. His muscled forearm rested on the white Formica. He wore his light brown hair and sideburns long. The red needle on my "handsome meter" bounced far to the right. Frank had come to visit a co-worker, but he soon returned and sought me out.

We "went steady" for two years, and spent a great deal of time at his parents' house. They were welcoming and easy-going, frequently inviting me for dinner. Frank and I did normal teenage activities: we went to drive-in movies, ate at fast-food restaurants, drank beer, and smoked a little weed. I didn't like marijuana because it made me sleepy and gave me the munchies. I had enough weight problems without being induced to rip open bags of Oreo cookies.

One night, Frank and I were watching TV; my parents had gone to bed. The kitchen and family room could be separated from the rest of the house by pulling closed mahogany Pella doors at one end of the room and by shutting a pocket door at the other. We closed both.

I stretched out on the edge of the rust colored couch. Frank snuggled next to me on his side. He leaned over and kissed me, his lips soft against mine. He tasted of Pepsi and smelled of Old Spice cologne. My fingers ran through the hair on the back of his neck. Each kiss became more ardent. His hand explored my body and then snuck under my halter top, playfully teasing each breast. Waves of pleasure rippled through me. His warm hand traced a path across my stomach and settled on the button of my shorts. Once undone, he worked the zipper down to expose pink bikini underwear. His fingers burrowed beneath the lace of my panties, and then slid between my legs. I lifted my body towards his caressing touch.

My heart stopped with the *whoosh* of the pocket door being opened.

Frank rocketed off the couch and fell back across me. His butt hid the splayed zipper of my white shorts. He threw one arm on the back of the sofa. We stared at the TV as if our present position was the norm for a couple viewing television.

Dad stepped into the kitchen and scrutinized the scene. All six feet of him stood ramrod-straight. I pictured a soldier on a mission, wearing night vision goggles. Infrared rays penetrating the darkness, taking in the landscape. He did an about-face and turned towards the faucet, lifted the handle, and shoved an empty glass under it. In a controlled voice he said, "It's time for Frank to leave."

Dad strode to the Pella doors and pushed them open. Then he marched across the aggregate floor and vanished into the bedroom.

Frank made a hasty exit. I zipped up my shorts, rearranged my halter top and rushed to my bedroom.

The next day Dad knocked on my bedroom door and stepped in. "I know you are having sex."

"I am not," I lied. The reality was I had done "it" once, several weeks prior. His relentless badgering eventually wore me down. I admitted to the one time, but my dad didn't believe me. Out of his mouth came words that have never left me.

"Sex is like eating peanuts, once you have one, you can't stop eating them."

Between sniffles, I swore to him I would never have sex again. I kept that promise for as long as a young horny gal could, but Dad was right. Those peanuts were addicting. One of the women I worked with allowed Frank and me to go to her place for our romantic trysts. By then I was on birth control pills. I had gone to my mother and told her the pills were necessary. She threatened to put a *chastity belt* on me. (I had to look that one up), but Mom relented, and made a doctor's appointment. Her revenge was to not warn me of the pelvic exam I would have to endure to get the pills.

On the day of my Junior Prom, Mom announced she had to go to the Emergency Room. Dad had been on a drunk and hadn't been home for days. It was not the first time he'd gone on a runner. Mom said she had to go to the hospital because her insides weren't working properly. She supposedly hadn't had a bowel movement for days. I knew the real reason for her trip to the hospital: she wanted to get Dad to come home. Mom practiced hypochondria, like her own mother, and used imaginary illnesses to manipulate. She asked me to call the bars to track Dad, and tell him where she was.

Mom's friend, Gracey, took her to the hospital. Gracey called me to say she had other obligations and had to leave Mom at the Emergency Room. Dad hadn't shown up, so I drove to the hospital. I stayed with her for hours. It was getting late, and I needed to get home to get ready for Prom. The doctors were still waiting for test results.

"You go home," she said as she patted my hand. "You have a big date tonight, and I'll be fine. Dad will most likely show up at some point, and if not, I can get a cab."

Since she didn't look ill, I left for home.

I finished applying my make-up and slipped on my beautiful sleeveless, floor-length dress. My tanned skin glowed dark next to the white lace atop the bright yellow liner. I liked the reflection in the mirror, and smiled to myself. I tingled with excitement for the evening ahead.

I heard the front door open and walked out to see my dad holding Mom's elbow, assisting her feeble attempt to walk. Though only 37 years of age, she appeared twice that. *She hadn't been this weak at the hospital.* Mom said, "Honey, you look so beautiful."

Dad spewed, "How could you leave your mother alone in the hospital? You only think of yourself. What kind of daughter are you?"

My fingers clenched into fists at my sides, nails cutting into palms. Dad had been gone for days, but now I was the one under attack. Face flushed and heart pounding, I yelled, "Mother told me to go home to get ready for Prom."

Dad continued to hurl obscenities and wave his arms as if he were conducting an orchestra. The theme of his tirade was my failings as a daughter. Mother disappeared meekly into her bedroom. Her not sticking up for me left my stomach in knots . . . betrayal knots. Tears ruined my make-up, leaving black mascara trails upon my cheeks. Frank was due at the house at any moment. I tried to paint on a new face over the splotchy red one that looked back at me in the mirror. The reflection wore no smile this time.

Nowadays on Facebook I see kids having pictures taken before their Prom, and I think *that's what it's supposed to be like.* Those kids look so happy and beautiful in their outfits. Some rites of passage you don't get a second chance at, and some memories never fade.

After two years, Frank and I went our separate ways. I met another young man through work, a co-worker named Tod. We hooked up at a party and began to date. Straight dark brown hair and mutton-chop sideburns embraced his face. I was eighteen and he was twenty-one. He was attractive, kind, and a gentle giant. He stood six foot, nine inches tall, and was accustomed to being noticed. Tod was very patient with the strangers who commented on his height. Many asked, "How's the weather up there?" He would chuckle like he'd never heard it before. I loved being with him, and felt safe within his arms.

Early in our dating, Tod wanted to take me to Santa Cruz for the weekend. I had never been out of town with a boyfriend. Since I was living with my parents, I asked their permission. It was given grudgingly.

The idea of traveling thrilled me. I felt free, and grown-up staying in a motel with Tod. We had a wonderful and magical weekend on the Boardwalk. I loved going on The Giant Dipper rollercoaster, eating ice-cream, and being on the beach. The evenings were romantic, under the stars, and listening to the sound of the surf. We sat on the sand, my back against the warmth of Tod's immense chest, mesmerized by the movement of the ocean. I could have stayed there forever.

When I returned home, my mom was friendly and asked about my weekend. I told her about places we had gone to eat and the fun we had had at the Boardwalk. She seemed happy for me.

Dad came home from work and could barely look at me. He didn't ask about my weekend, but Mom had a few more questions regarding my trip. I started to answer, and Dad exploded. He threw ice-cubes into the sink, and slammed his glass down onto the counter. He turned to me and sneered. "You just have to rub my nose in it, don't you?"

"Rub your nose in what?"

"That you had sex this past weekend."

"What?" I said. "I wasn't rubbing your nose in anything. I was just answering Mom's questions about Santa Cruz."

"You were rubbing my nose in it," he yelled.

"Tod lives in an apartment. Do you think I have to leave town to make love to him? You are being ridiculous." I stomped out of the kitchen, and went into my bedroom, slamming the door. I flounced onto the bed, fuming.

I wanted a normal life. To have wonderful experiences, and not have them tainted by outrageous accusations. I yearned for a regular relationship with my dad, but I knew it couldn't be.

One evening, Tod dropped me off at the house after a date. It was late. I opened the front door to find my dad waiting for me. He was drunk. He pushed the door closed and pinned me against it, towering above me. Mom was nowhere to be seen. "What's wrong?" I asked, smelling alcohol. His 80 proof breath burned my eyes.

"Nothing," he slurred. "Did you . . . have a good date?"

"Yes," I said, as he leaned in to kiss me on the lips. I turned my head and pushed him away. "No Dad," I said in disgust. I escaped to my room and locked the door. *Would it never end?*

Tod and I continued to date. To commemorate our one year anniversary, Tod bought champagne. He popped the cork and it bounced off the ceiling of his living room. He disappeared into the kitchen and brought back two glasses for our toast. As I was about to take a sip, I noticed something at the bottom of my goblet. It was a ring. He lowered himself to one knee and asked me to be his wife. Tears of joy cascaded over my cheeks. We laughed, hugged, kissed.

Tod drove me home, and I went straight into my room. Mom opened the door and came in.

Grinning and exuberant, I waved my hand. The ring sparkled in the light, a beautiful heart-shaped diamond solitaire. Mother's face screwed up in horror. "How could you? You are too young to get married. What about school?"

My engagement news did not unfold like a Hallmark moment. Most of the significant events in my life didn't come close to what was depicted on television. *Why was my life so different from what was portrayed on TV?* My mother had married at twenty, the same age I planned to wed, but I was too young. *Go figure.* In truth, my mom didn't want me leaving home. She had no desire to be the only female in the house.

Tod and I were engaged for a year. During that time I saw resignation come over Dad. He knew I was moving out and came to accept Tod, in his way.

I couldn't wait for the freedom. I wanted to create a safe haven to live and love my husband. Miracles do happen, and I finally got my Hallmark moment . . . our wedding.

9

Carson City

*E*very person who sits with me is special, but certain reads have seized my heart and lingered. Divine intervention connected me to specific people, and that held true at the psychic fair in Carson City, Nevada.

The Sherris, from Wings Over Soul, had told me about this festival. I booked it and made travel arrangements immediately.

At the same time I learned of the Carson City fair, a serendipitous event occurred at my Writer's Group. I met Molly, a talented beautiful young woman roughly my daughter's age. During the evening it came out that I did tarot readings. Molly's face lit up. "Really? Some time ago I wrote a story called Erin, The Tarot Reader, and now I'm meeting one in the flesh."

"You can't make this stuff up," I said, shaking my head. "Have you ever had a reading yourself?"

"No, strange as it might be. I did all of my research for the story on the Internet."

"Well, we can't have that," I said. "Would you like to get a tarot card reading?"

Molly nodded. "That would be awesome!"

Just before leaving the meeting, we made arrangements for her to come to my home.

Days prior to Molly's reading, a strange thing happened. I was walking toward my kitchen when the pungent odor of permanent hair solution invaded my nostrils. There was no logical reason for the smell since I'd last permed my hair in the 1980s. I sensed the smell was tied to spirit, but whose?

An hour before Molly's appointment, the stink of perm solution stopped me in mid-stride. I had a hunch the scent was connected to Molly's visit.

Molly barely had time to get in the door, before I started in. "I need to ask you something. I've been smelling perm solution this week. Do you have a grandmother figure who has crossed over, who permed her hair? I feel she belongs to you."

Molly appeared startled. "Yes, I did have a grandmother who often got her hair permed."

"Well, she's been with me this past week, and knew you were coming for a reading. I'm sure she's with us now."

"That's wild," Molly said, peering around the room as if trying to spot her. "I'm glad she's here."

Molly's reading was fun and interesting. She received a lot of messages about moving stuck energy and speaking her truth. During a pause, I heard a voice within that said, *Ask her.* I *knew* what they wanted me to ask, but my rational mind balked. They wanted me to invite her to the Carson City festival. An obvious concern was that we hardly knew each other. Why would I ask a stranger to spend the weekend with me? I didn't understand it, but knew I had to honor the message. I interrupted the reading, and asked Molly if she might be interested in going to Carson City to assist me. I explained she could travel with me if she wished, and stay in my hotel room. I thought first-hand knowledge of a festival might prove helpful to her story, and her assistance there would be a great help.

Molly's enthusiasm showed on her face. "Sounds like fun."

On the day of the Carson City fair, Molly and I woke early, ate breakfast, and made our way to the venue. Situated next to a tree filled park, the building had the floorboards and expanse of a gymnasium, but seemed newer and cleaner. Several vendors were busy setting up their booths; I waved to a few I knew. After time spent searching the walls, I located a sign that indicated my 10 X 10 home for the weekend. Molly and I made quick work of setting up my booth. I enjoyed the extra help.

Seeing the room come to life was exciting, and the energy was palpable. I had been told my booth had a cozy and inviting look, and I had to agree. Molly sat at the front table ready to welcome customers, and I stood by her side. Usually, it took a little time before I booked my first reading, but not this day. A petite woman in her mid to late thirties with sandy blonde hair approached the table. "Can I get a reading?"

"Sure," I said and introduced myself. Her name was Tina and she had a slight Australian accent that had worn thin from her years in the States.

Once Tina was seated, I explained that if she were agreeable, I would start with a soul read. It allowed me to "ground in" and connect with her while her soul selected the cards it wished to discuss.

Looking over her card choices, I was moved to begin with The Waiting Game. Bordered in purple, the center of the card held an hour glass, and within that grew a tree. The roots of the tree appeared in the bottom half of the glass, and the trunk rose through the narrow waist, giving way to branches and green leaves in the upper portion. Radiating circles surrounded the outside of the hour glass and a man walked atop the circles.

I flipped the card toward Tina and said, "This card speaks to me of stuck energy, energy that may be ready to move forward. You've been working on making something happen, and you've been waiting for it to come to fruition. Does this make sense to you?"

Tina nodded her head and tears began to roll down her cheeks. "I've been waiting and waiting."

In a hushed voice I asked, "What have you been waiting for, honey?"

"A baby," Tina said. "We have one child who's ten, and I know I'm blessed, but my husband and I so wanted another child. It feels like it's not going to happen."

I knew Tina's devastation first-hand, and my own feelings flooded back. I, too, had thought I would not be able to get pregnant. When I turned 35, my biological clock sounded an alarm, not a gentle buzzing, more like an air-raid siren. I had never been pregnant, and had no idea if my body could sustain a life. My husband was seven years older than I, so we both had a wary eye trained on our fertility meters. We decided to try to add to our family before it was too late.

For months, I took my temperature daily and used ovulation kits to know when I was the most fertile. It was like a science project. My husband and I worked diligently on our baby making homework. I hated to admit it, but making love at "just the right time," sure took the fun out of the assignment. Our efforts paid off, and I was ecstatic when I finally missed my period. I peed on a stick and took the "at home" pregnancy test to confirm we were truly going to be parents.

Family members were happy for us, my Mother at the forefront. She had thought she would never be a grandma.

Three months into my pregnancy, I was suddenly struck with pains that radiated around my belly. I didn't know what was happening, so I grabbed a pregnancy book to research my symptoms. It said I could be losing the baby. Kent and I rushed to the emergency room, where the doctors echoed what the book had already warned. They advised we would just have to wait and see. Paralyzed with fear and totally powerless, I took to my bed. *How could this be happening?* All I could do was pray the baby would stay inside me and grow.

While in bed, the next morning an intense pain grabbed my midsection and doubled me over. I stumbled my way toward the toilet. Just as I collapsed onto the seat, water gushed from my body. I looked into the toilet bowl and saw a tiny form. I tried to force my mind to think. I was bleeding, scared, and by myself. I got a Kotex pad and put it in my underwear. I looked away as I fished into the bowl for the fetus. My hope was that doctors could run tests to discover why I hadn't been able to keep my baby. I gently placed the little figure into a plastic baggie and slid it into a brown paper bag.

Sobbing, I called my husband at work. "I lost the baby and I'm going to the emergency room." He tried to comfort me and told me he would meet me there. I had no memory of the drive to the hospital.

The emergency room staff admitted me right away. I told one of the nurses what was in my precious brown paper sack, and she patted my arm and then eased the bag from my grasp. I could hear whispers amongst the staff, and was treated tenderly.

A nurse informed me a doctor would have to perform a surgical procedure called a D and C. I had no idea what it was. She further explained the doctor would go in and clean the lining of my uterus. With my legs spread in the most vulnerable position, I stared up at the ceiling tiles. Tears

147

trickled across my temples, and into my ears. The doctor removed all remnants of my pregnancy. A great sorrow followed, permeating my being.

I missed work for a week and cried everyday. I had never experienced so much grief. While growing up, I'd learned crying was a sign of weakness. It never proved beneficial to be so exposed. However, in Al Anon, I'd given myself permission to be human, and to feel my feelings. Sadness coursed through me unchecked.

I had been broadsided by this terrible loss, as was my husband and family. My body still looked and vibrated like it carried a baby, but I knew the truth. Women went to term and had healthy babies all the time, why not me? Maybe I was too old and couldn't have a baby. I was devastated and grief covered me like a shroud.

Now Tina sat before me crying, wondering if she would ever conceive again. I shared how I, too, believed that I might never get pregnant again after the loss of my baby. "I feel compelled to tell you the rest of my story, and I'm going to speak frankly, if it's okay with you?"

"Please do," Tina said, as she dried her tears.

"After losing our baby, I had an appointment with my OB/GYN, as instructed by the emergency room doctor. I was amazed to learn my OB/GYN was the head of the fertility clinic. It was comforting to talk to him, and I affectionately called him Dr. Love. The doctor advised that I wait three months before trying to get pregnant again, so I could heal. He also said I had a tipped uterus, which might make it more difficult for me to get pregnant. Dr. Love explained that 80% of the fertility problems he saw was due to the sperm not getting to where it needed to go. This happened because women frequently got up to pee after intercourse, so the sperm just ran out. The doctor said I might think him crazy, but he knew his next suggestion worked. Immediately after having sex, I was to get my butt up against the headboard and my feet up against the wall, and stay that way for twenty minutes. Aided by gravity, the sperm had no problems swimming to their desired location. His method did sound ridiculous, but I so wanted a baby."

I told Tina I had *needed* to tell her this crazy story, and hoped it could be of some use in her own life. I said, "My husband and I waited the three months, and I looked comical doing the bicycle kick against the headboard, but it worked. At Christmas, I surprised my husband with a card, congratulating him on his impending fatherhood. Nine months later a healthy baby girl arrived. Katie is twenty-two now. I'll be forever grateful to Dr. Love and his unorthodox method."

Tina smiled and thanked me for the story. "It gives me hope, and I'm so glad you told me."

We discussed our experiences, and how sex could become a chore when you were on a mission to make a baby. The various kits, and the daily taking of your temperature before you get out of bed, could wear on a woman. Sex was much more enjoyable when it was spontaneous.

Tina had also drawn the Awareness card. The border was black and in the center were the head and shoulders of a magician. He wore a fancy head piece. His crown chakra was aglow, as if something from the heavens had struck it.

"Tina, this card is about you working with your higher power and creating the life you wish to have. It's about manifesting your desires." I explained it was my belief that if we came from a place of faith, and believed our desire was already on its way, a positive vibration was created that allowed us to receive. At least, that's how manifesting worked in my life.

It seemed Tina needed a shift to take place, especially with trying to manifest a baby. A positive attitude and a belief a baby was on its way to her might be advantageous to her cause.

She said, "I have not been in a good place, and I've definitely had a 'lack of' mentality. I want to work on changing this." She told me she and her husband had had several tests, and the doctor said there was nothing physically preventing them from conceiving again.

As our time together ended, I was glad to see Tina had a smile on her face. Hugging, we said our goodbyes.

The level of intimacy that I'm allowed to experience through tarot readings is truly a gift. I could never have imagined the blessings that would come my way, or the connections I would make when I first considered learning the tarot.

As the day went on, I got the impression that being in Carson City had only been about meeting Tina, but I was wrong.

10

Another One

$\mathcal{I}$t was 4:00 p.m. on Saturday, quitting time at the Carson City fair. The day had flown by. Molly and I headed back to our hotel room so I could decompress before dinner.

Once in the room, we kicked off our shoes and flounced onto the queen beds. I inhaled several times; I was tired and a little goofy after a full day of readings. It always took awhile for me to shift gears and come out of the fog, to plug back into the "thinking" part of my brain. Readings and psychometry seemed to use some other part of my mind.

The more readings I did, the less I retained of them, so I came up with a strategy that helped me remember what occurred. I used a writing tablet when I held an object of the clients, and made a list of what came through. I went "old school" and used carbon paper, so I could keep a copy for myself. This allowed me to chart my growth and recall what information had been validated.

I reached for the stack of carbon copies I had brought back from the fair. As I scanned the lists, Molly said she had some questions for me. Sitting in a 10 X 10 booth made for an intimate setting, and she could hear much of the readings. Molly asked, "What happens internally when you do psychometry and hold an object?"

No one had ever asked me that question before. "Well . . . let's see. I close my eyes and I focus on a tall grey wall inside my head, between my brows. Water cascades over the top of the wall. I ask my guides to 'hook me up' and I look for images that fall from above. Sometimes I won't see anything, but I'll hear a word or a phrase."

Molly grinned. "There was a moment today when you were doing psychometry, when I wanted to yell out *'eggcup.'* You were trying to describe the object to your customer, and I knew what you were talking about, but I kept my mouth shut." This sent the two of us into fits of laughter.

"I wish you had, I was struggling," I said between giggles. "At times, I go brain-dead while doing readings. It's as if my thinking mind disconnects. I can see the image, but the name of the object won't come. I told the woman I'd seen these things in the movies, where a wealthy person eats a soft-boiled egg from the shell, while it sits in this *holder*. Thank goodness she finally understood, and guessed *eggcup*."

Propping myself up against the headboard, I said, "What I found interesting, was that the woman had just asked the cards if she was ever going to travel again. The reading revealed, at present, she had too many items on her plate, but once she finished with her commitments, she would travel. She validated the information by saying she was in the middle of a kitchen remodel, and an outdoor landscaping project. In addition, her husband had health issues. She enjoyed hearing she would travel in the future. She explained that *eggcups* were significant to her because she had purchased two in Sweden as souvenirs. Her secret desire to return to Sweden had prompted the travel question."

"That is interesting." Molly said. "What else did you get for her?"

I grabbed my carbon copies and sorted through them until I found the woman's list. "When I held her ring, I got *little white dog* and *fire pit*. She told me the dog was Daisy, her Bichon Frise. She said she had just visited her son in Southern California. During her stay she had made S'mores with her grandkids over the outdoor *fire pit*. So that was a fun reading for me, and I know she got a kick out of it, too."

Molly said, "As the woman walked away, she kept shaking her head and repeating, 'I don't believe she got *eggcups*.' I got a laugh out of that."

"Me too," I said. It had been an enjoyable day.

Molly and I changed for dinner. We needed food, and wanted to check out some of the local casinos. We couldn't stay out too late since we had to get up early for the second day of the fair.

Sundays were typically less busy, so I urged Molly to investigate some of the other booths. The morning saw a handful of customers milling around, so I was delighted when an older, petite woman approached me. She asked the cost of a reading, and when I told her she agreed to get one. She had never had a reading before—another virgin.

Introductions were made, and Lois took the seat across from me. She had short, greasy iron-grey hair. She wore it straight and parted in the middle. Her hair hung listless above her shoulders. A barrette on each side of her forehead pinned back short bangs, forming a mini-curtain of hair above her brows. There was a childlike quality to her, but none of the enthusiasm of youth. I sensed she kept all emotions locked in a vault and she'd long since lost the combination.

I explained how I did my readings, and that I believed she would pick the cards her soul wanted to discuss. Lois said, "Yeah, to whatever you just said. I didn't understand any of it."

I wasn't quite sure how to respond. "Would you like me to repeat it?"

"No, no, . . . go ahead," Lois said with a wave of her hand.

I asked her to select her cards. The two I wanted to discuss first were Spiritual Union and Memories of Love. "I feel these two cards are bound together. A person of significance, or someone whom you had a special bond with, has either passed away or the relationship has ended. I'm given a sense of wistfulness. Like you're yearning for something to be different. Does this mean anything to you?"

Eyes wide, Lois stared at me, as if frozen. I continued to search her face for any sign of acknowledgement, but she remained statue-like. To break the silence I said, "I've lost many friends and family over the years. I went through a seven year period where I lost six loved ones. It began with my husband's suicide."

Her sudden movement startled me. Lois shot an arm towards me, her index finger pointed at my heart. "I can do you one better. My son committed suicide!"

157

Taken aback by her reaction, I thought: *What an odd thing to say, as if it were a competition.*

Lois' lips were held tightly in a grimace, and her eyes filled with tears.

"I'm so sorry you lost your son. How long ago was it?"

Hunched over the table so only I could hear, Lois said, "Two years."

How long had it been for me? Eleven years and counting since I first learned of my husband's suicide. At times, it felt fresh, like an open wound, raw and ugly. When it had happened, my immediate concern had been how to break the news to my daughter and step-kids. My words would set the tone for years to come, so I wanted to speak with care. My message to the kids was that suicide shouldn't be a secret, and was nothing to be ashamed of. I didn't want Kent's death to become a forbidden subject. Kent had been under the influence of alcohol and drugs, and was troubled and depressed. He had made a horrible decision with far-reaching effects. A decision he never would have made had he been lucid.

Thank God for the friends and family that helped us get through the "Year of Firsts," the first

Christmas, Thanksgiving, and all the birthdays without him. I was Zombie-like in the beginning. How I worked, took care of my daughter, and our house, was a mystery to me.

My daughter and I went to counseling, and learned ways to heal and cope. Even with the counseling, it took ten months to feel like I had any spark of life. Driving home from work, listening to a song on the radio, I began to sing along. I stopped; my own voice stunned me. I hadn't sung since Kent had died. That was my first jolt of hope. As if unseen paddles had been placed on my chest, sending electric shocks to restart my heart.

Our family struggled for many years to get to some kind of "new normal." It was inconceivable when another member of our family took his life. It hurled all of us back into a very dark place. I could still hear Katie's cry of anguish when she learned that her Uncle, her dad's brother, had spilled his own blood. It happened in the same month, seven years after Kent's passing. Depression and alcoholism had claimed another sweet soul.

I was all too familiar with suicide and its aftermath, so it was no surprise that Lois now sat at my table. Another one, among the many I'd met, who'd experienced the gut-wrenching loss of a loved one by suicide. Many tools had assisted me in my grief, so I said, "I understand the pain and loss that comes when a family member takes their own life. Counseling was so helpful to me after my husband died. Have you had any counseling or been to a bereavement group?"

Lois shook her head and answered curtly. "I donate to Suicide Prevention, but I won't go to any group or counseling."

"How is your husband handling your son's death?" I asked.

"Oh, he says he's fine, but I know he's not. We've been together over 40 years now, so I read him like a book."

"Are the two of you able to comfort each other, and talk about the loss of your son?"

"No, my husband and I never talk about it. It's an unwritten rule." Lois shifted uncomfortably in her chair. "We moved from the East Coast to Nevada. No one here knew my son, so it was pointless to speak of him anyway."

My heart ached for her. I couldn't imagine not talking about my departed loved ones. I said, "I'm sorry you don't talk about your son, it brings me a measure of peace to talk about my husband, and others who have passed. I talk to all my loved ones who have crossed over, I feel closer to them."

Her face scrunched up, and she gave me a quizzical look.

"My husband suffered from depression and he didn't reach out for any help at the end. I believe that led to his suicide."

Lois nodded. "My son also suffered from depression. It was hard to watch him struggle with it, and not be able to help him." Lois looked down at the table, and took a deep breath and exhaled audibly. "He was such a sweet boy," she whispered. As if a door had been thrown open, she proceeded to tell me about her son and his interests. In the telling, a glimmer of a smile touched her lips.

When she finished with what she needed to say, I said, "He sounds very special."

"He was."

I asked if she wanted me to continue with her reading, and she nodded. The remaining cards spoke of her taking care of herself: body, mind and spirit. Being honest with herself was another focus. I encouraged her to reach out to someone, whether it be a girlfriend or a professional, to talk about her son. I knew my departed loved ones continued to watch over me, just as Lois was watched over by her son.

As she stood to leave, Lois said, "I never expected to talk about my son today. I came in here by accident. I saw the sign for the fair from the road, and something made me turn the car around."

After giving her a hug, I said, "Well, I'm glad you decided to walk in, and that you chose to spend some time with me today."

She gave a slight nod, turned her petite frame, and walked slowly out of the building.

I first thought that the purpose of coming to Carson City had been about the Saturday reading with Tina, the woman who feared she couldn't get pregnant again. Now I knew there had been two reasons; Lois was the second.

11

Meeting Dänna

I've been more consciously aware of synchronistic events since I committed myself to living an intuitive life. Others might call them coincidences, but I don't believe there are any. Seemingly random acts gain in significance in hindsight, and often in the moment they happen.

One such act was the need to get a reading just prior to my first Healing Arts Festival. I wanted some clarity around my tarot business, and was hoping to bolster my waning courage. A woman I met on the Awaken Your Spirit Cruise of 2014 had spoken highly of Nancy, a psychic medium. I'd already had one reading from her and I looked forward to another.

We made a date to connect by phone, since she lived out of state. Nancy had me repeat my full name, three times. This was how she "tuned in" and began her readings. Nancy's voice was low and calming. She said, "It feels like you are owning what you create in a different way, in a much more confident way. In the past, there may have been judgement about what you created and what you brought into your life. Now instead of judgement you view things with a curiosity and interest. You appear to be very flexible with new people who come into your life, and you have a solid foundation that seems comfortable." Nancy paused. "Does this make sense to you?"

"Yes, it does, and I've done a lot of work to get here."

"Well, good for you. Do you have any questions for me?" Nancy asked.

"I do. Can you please tell me what you see around my tarot business. I plan to have a booth and work my first festival in a month."

"Let me look at this for a second." Nancy continued. "I see the festival being a very positive experience. In addition, I see there will be an interview. There is some local radio or Internet TV station that is into the tarot and alternative thinking. This will lead not only to clients, but will also establish some helpful partnerships."

"You see me—being interviewed?" I asked. *Nancy can't be right on this one.*

"Yes," Nancy said. "She looks like she's local and has a following. She doesn't appear to be very far from you. You may want to Google it, and see if there are any local stations that are into the paranormal."

"You seeing an interview has thrown me, but it sure is intriguing to think about."

The rest of the reading gave me some insight into my abilities and Nancy told me I might do something other than the tarot, something that would be even more fun for me. Her readings always gave me food for thought.

Five months later I was doing a "Day of Readings" at the Journey Center in Shingle Springs. The center, located forty-five minutes from my home, housed various healers. Synchronistic circumstances had led me up Highway 50 to this treasured facility.

The sequence of events started rolling when I was compelled to tell one woman at my dentist's office that I was starting a new tarot reading business. I gave her my business card, and she told me she was into "these kind of things." Mind you, ten women worked in that office, but I only felt driven to give one person my business card, and

I wasn't even sure of her name. I later learned it was Lisa. She eventually got a reading from me, and asked me to do a Ladies Tarot Party at her home.

One day over coffee, I mentioned to Lisa that I had a strange compulsion to try acupuncture. For no apparent reason, I had a desire to experience it. Lisa informed me her sister was an Acupuncturist who worked out of the Journey Center. I met Lisa's sister, and I also met a wonderful massage therapist. I clicked with both women. The two ran the Journey Center for the owner. The Acupuncturist suggested that I put up a flyer on their Community Board to promote my tarot readings, and to consider doing a day of readings there. Those synchronistic happenings are what led to the "Day of Readings" and my association with the Journey Center.

I was at the Journey Center and had just finished my first reading. I had some time to kill before my next six scheduled readings, so I walked around the large office space. I was drawn to the Community Board. Push-pins held business cards of local entrepreneurs and healers. My gaze landed on a postcard, and written across the top in bold letters was: Where Science Meets The Spirit World. It gave information about Paranormal Connection TV, where to watch, and how to contact them. It showed a picture of the host, a beautiful blonde woman named Dänna Wilberg. I stared at the postcard and heard: *This is it.* I knew Dänna

Wilberg was the person I was to contact, and who could manifest Nancy's premonition into a reality. I took a picture of the postcard with my iPhone.

When I got home from the Journey Center, I went to my office and got on the computer to learn more about Paranormal Connection TV. I found that many of Dänna's interviews were on YouTube. I watched several of them. She had such an easy-going manner, and it felt like *this was it*.

I sent an email to Paranormal Connection TV. I introduced myself and said I was a local tarot reader, and I was interested in getting on the show. I wasn't quite sure how one went about doing that, but I would appreciate it if someone would contact me.

One week later I received a call, I never expected Dänna to be on the phone. I thought I might be contacted by someone else from Paranormal Connection TV, but never the host. We had a delightful conversation, and I learned she had many talents. Not only a host, but a published author and filmmaker. She had impressive abilities. I told her the story of my psychic reading and the synchronicities that had led me to her.

While on the phone, Dänna said, "I would love for you to be on the show. We are supposed to start filming again in October, but I'm not sure if that is going to happen. All of my wonderful crew volunteer their time, and I may be losing one of them, so things are up in the air at present. As we get closer, I'll call and let you know if the show is going to return. I love doing the show and hope it continues."

Not long after our conversation, I received an email informing me that I would be on the show. I needed to report to the studio on October 17th for the taping. She would be doing several back-to-back interviews with various guests.

My first thought was to call my mom, but I couldn't, as she had died several years earlier. The sad part was that many of the people I wanted to share my excitement with were gone. So I gazed up to the heavens and thanked them all for watching over me. If any of them had a hand in what was happening, I was grateful. I called my daughter and a few girlfriends to let them know of my good fortune.

Arriving at the studio, I was thrilled, nervous, and very curious. My stomach went into an agitated flutter. Dänna and her crew were very welcoming. I got a tour of the control booth, and checked out the cameras, and the lighting. Two chairs and a table were on the stage. The setting had a homey vibe.

My turn came. One of the crew placed a microphone under my shirt, whereupon I grabbed it and pulled it through the top of my blouse. The crew member fastened the mic to my neckline, and

I took my seat. I remember Dänna introducing me, and then in the next instant, she asked if there was anything else I wanted to say to the viewers. Our thirty minutes were up. *What?* It felt like an out-of-body experience, and I didn't remember what I had said. When I watched the show later, it seemed like someone else had done the interview. It was surreal. The end product went beyond my expectations. I had done a decent job of explaining my readings and how I had gotten interested in the tarot. The astounding part was not being conscious of the time passing.

I thanked Dänna for the rare opportunity, and told her I'd be forever in her debt. She posted the interview on YouTube. Now prospective customers could view it, but, more importantly, my daughter had a living memory of me. Katie would be able to hear and see me talking about a passion.

The interview aired three times in November of 2016. I was peacefully sleeping at 5:30 a.m. during the final airing on November 5th. A little after 6:00 a.m., I received a phone call. I don't keep the ringer on as a rule, but my daughter had stayed the night at a friend's. When Katie didn't sleep at home, my phone stayed on. I groggily answered and learned it was a woman who had just watched the show and wanted a reading. I asked if she might call me back around 9:30 a.m. The woman apologized, and said she didn't expect anyone to answer. I told her about my 22 year old daughter not being at home, and she understood why I had answered.

Sleep would not find me again, so I got up. My plan for the morning was to get a meal into the crock pot so my daughter and I could enjoy it that evening. While seasoning the meat and vegetables, information dropped in through one of the "clairs." I heard: *She may talk about being suicidal. What are you going to do? Who would you need to call?* I knew the information was about the woman who was supposed to call at 9:30 a.m.

Since I was forewarned, I went over various scenarios in my head and what I would say. I gathered some phone numbers dealing with suicide prevention and stood at the ready.

At exactly 9:30 a.m. the call came. Marilyn introduced herself and again apologized for the early call. "I really thought no one would answer and it would go to voicemail. I was watching your interview on Paranormal Connection TV, and knew I needed to act because I've been so depressed. I recognized I couldn't sit in my misery any longer." There was a brief silence before she continued. "My daughter and I aren't speaking, and sometimes I get so despondent that I think of ways of killing myself."

So there it was, the talk of suicide. While listening to Marilyn, I sensed she had not actual plans to hurt herself.

I said, "Information dropped in this morning, and I *heard* you were going to talk about suicide."

"That came to you just from the brief call this morning?"

"Yes," I said.

I heard Marilyn's sharp intake of breath before she let loose. "I want you to know, that I am an 88 year old psychologist. I've run many a bereavement group in my day. I may think of ways of ending my life, but I'm certainly not going to act on them."

I knew she was telling the truth, and the fact she was 88 supported her statement. "That's wonderful to hear," I said. "My husband committed suicide, and I know the devastation and fallout from someone taking their own life. Friends and family are forever altered. I'm glad you understand the impact on family, and have no intentions of harming yourself."

"I'm sorry about your husband," Marilyn said. "As I stated, I am aware of the pain suicide causes, and won't put my family through it."

We agreed to meet in three days for an hour reading. I asked if she needed the reading sooner, but Marilyn assured me she would be fine. Before we got off the phone, she said, "I know you are the person I'm supposed to talk to."

My higher power sends individuals my way, and it's always fascinating to meet them. I have faith that I'm supposed to spend time with each

.t for the life of me, I was stumped on
.ld help a psychologist. Yet there were no
.ences, and I had been going through my
period of not getting along with my daughter.
₁ knew Marilyn and I had a connection.

My conflicts with Katie had caused me to do a tremendous amount of soul-searching regarding being an "only" parent, and the dynamics of the mother/daughter relationship. I thought the key to having a wonderful relationship with my daughter was by being a sober Mom. I wanted our connection to look *nothing* like the one that had existed between my mother and me. Boy, was I wrong.

Katie was twenty-two years old and couldn't wait to move out and get as far away from me as possible. In her eyes, I suddenly knew nothing, while just as suddenly she knew it all. I appeared just as toxic to Katie as my mother had been to me, and she told me so on more than one occasion.

From the beginning, Katie was loved and wanted. Like most parents, I tried to protect her, but I became somewhat over-protective after Kent died. The thought of something happening to Katie, especially when she began to experiment with drugs and alcohol, terrified me. Moms worry, and any remote possibility that I could lose Katie kept me emotionally unbalanced for a time.

Recently, my daughter had found it necessary to let me know all the ways I had failed her as a parent. The list was cringe-worthy, and there were elements of truth in her observations. My karma roped around full circle. The pain and angst I'd heaped on my mother came back to haunt me. I remembered the hateful things I had slung at my own mother, and now realized she may have experienced the same heart-wrenching pains I knew each time Katie and I fought.

The early years had been good. After Kent died, she wouldn't sleep in her bed, so she snuggled with me for six months. It was never a question of love between us, the issue was more about *like*. It seemed she didn't like me as a person. My hope was that someday, as adults, we would have the easy relationship I had envisioned while Katie was cocooned in my womb. Several girlfriends advised me that from 18 to 23 it might not be so good, but Katie would come back around after that. I was banking on their expertise.

I'm aware of all the psychological lingo about how kids need to individuate and become their own person, and consequently push parents away. Having that knowledge didn't make me feel any better when Katie and I were at odds. Because of my own mother, I strove to parent better than I had been parented, and to come from a loving place and nurture. My job was to let Katie go with love. I prayed that one day, she too, would reflect and gain some insight into her mother.

Not surprising that I now had a reading with a woman who was having issues with her daughter. On the day of Marilyn's reading, I opened the door to a stylish older woman. Her hair was the color of a flame and fell past her shoulders. She reminded me a bit of Endora on "Bewitched." To look as good as she did at 88, she must have had some work done. Wrinkles were scarce. As I said hello, I tilted back my head to give my neck a somewhat firmer appearance.

I showed Marilyn to my reading room and explained how I worked. She had an antsy demeanor and kept fidgeting in her chair. In a hurried fashion, Marilyn selected her cards. Most people took their time, and picked each card with scrutiny and care. She took a much different approach. When I spoke about each card, Marilyn shrugged her shoulders and said she wasn't sure if she could relate to them. I'd never experienced a sitter with an attitude like hers.

I asked. "Is there a specific question you would like to ask of the cards?"

Marilyn leaned forward and said, "Can I *not* ask a question, and just talk to you, and tell you what's going on between me and one of my daughters?"

"Sure," I could see why she hadn't been interested in her reading, she had her own agenda. Getting her story out was the priority.

Marilyn patted her hair to make sure all was in place and began. "My daughter isn't talking to me right now. I gave her $15,000.00 on the condition she build a cottage for me to live in, on some property she was buying. Well, she ended up not buying the land, so I requested she return the $15,000.00. Her recollection regarding the money was far different from mine. She believed I had just given her the money, no strings attached. Anger got the best of me. I wrote a letter saying I was going to deduct the $15,000 from her inheritance. That's when she stopped speaking to me. Now I'm just sick over the whole mess."

"I'm so sorry you two aren't talking. I haven't been getting along with my daughter either, so I understand your sadness."

Tears rolled down Marilyn's cheeks. "My daughter and I travel in the same social circles and go to the same church, so there is no one I can talk to about this issue. I don't even care about the money anymore. I just want my daughter to talk to me again. Being estranged from her feels as though I'm slowly bleeding out. When I saw you on Paranormal Connection TV, I thought you might be someone I could talk to."

"That's kind of you to say. Don't you know of someone in your professional circle who could assist you?"

"No," she said.

"Does your daughter know that you don't care about the money, or is she under the impression it's still being deducted from her inheritance? Also, did you do anything legally to have it deducted in your will?"

While dabbing at her tears, Marilyn said, "My daughter has no idea that I don't care about the money anymore, and no, I didn't do anything legally."

"Why don't you tell your daughter you've changed your mind about the money, and tell her how important she is to you? This might be a way to shift the energy and get it moving in a more positive direction. Your daughter may still choose not to speak to you, but at least you'll have said what's in your heart and mind. As you know, we have no control over the behavior of another adult. Whatever you send, keep it simple and to the point. I wouldn't rehash all the old stuff. Also, I'd suggest doing a self-check, and be very clear that you've truly let go of the $15,000.00."

Marilyn assured me she didn't care about the money, and she just wanted to send a text to her daughter. I gave her several suggestions about what she might say, and she seemed to like them, but she still appeared uptight. I asked, "Do you want me to write something down for you?"

Marilyn's whole demeanor changed. "It would be so wonderful if you would do that."

I took some time to write a simple and heartfelt statement from Marilyn to her daughter, and I handed it to her. "Let me know if this is okay, or if you would like to add or subtract any of the wording."

Marilyn took a minute to read it. "It's perfect. Thank you so much for writing this and for seeing me today. I feel so much better now."

As Marilyn walked down my driveway, I sent out healing prayers for both our daughters and ourselves.

It was one of my most unusual appointments because it had nothing to do with a reading. It was about service to others, and how intricate and binding the mother/daughter relationship was, no matter the age.

12

Mom's Passing

*M*y second appearance at the Healing Arts Festival blessed me with another poignant reading. One that involved mothers and daughters, yet again.

A cheerful buxom woman with short curly black hair approached my front table and asked for a reading. I ushered her through dark framed privacy screens to my haven. We made our introductions, and Ruth told me she had never had a reading.

I laughed. "You would not believe how often I hear that. I'm a magnet for first-timers."

As Ruth began to select her cards, her hand stopped in mid-motion. "I don't want to pick the wrong cards."

"You'll pick the ones your soul wants to discuss," I said.

Ruth passed each card to me, and I placed them into a spread. Gazing upon one particular card, I was suddenly overcome with emotion. "I'm sorry, Ruth. I don't usually feel like this, but I want to cry." I turned the Sacrifice card towards her. "I'm feeling emotional when I look at this card. This card represents being a caregiver for a family member, or the person does the work professionally. My emotions are taking me back to a time when my mother was in poor health. I sense your card may be tied to a mother figure. Does this make sense to you?"

"Yes, it does." Ruth picked up the card and examined it. She looked at me and continued. "I was my mother's caregiver and she passed away six months ago. It was horrible to watch her weaken and waste away. I'm struggling with what to do with myself now that I'm not providing full-time care. That's the reason I wanted a reading today."

"I understand your struggle because you also selected the Passion Ignited card." The card showed a woman in a bright colored robe with her eyes closed and head tilted back. A look of rapture painted her face, and a fire glowed near her heart chakra.

I turned the card towards her. "This card is about finding an activity or hobby that fills you with passion. You may have to look back to your childhood, or recall an activity where you were so absorbed, you lost all track of time. Does anything come to mind?"

Ruth bit her lip while thinking and then her faced relaxed. "Horseback riding," she said. "I haven't ridden since I was a kid, but I sure loved it and spent hours doing it. While brushing the horses, I escaped into my own little world. They are such beautiful creatures."

"That may be something you take up again since you have the time." We took several minutes brainstorming other activities that sparked Ruth's passion.

I finished her read just as the timer beeped. We were out of time, but I had promised her I would do psychometry. "What would you like me to hold?"

She began to twist a ring off her finger. Ruth dropped a silver band with tiny embedded diamonds into my left hand. I closed my eyes and the first thing I heard was *grandmother - very close*. I wrote the words on my tablet. Next, an image of a *Ritz Cracker* appeared. I added it to my list.

Ruth interrupted me. "Now I'm going to cry."

181

I glanced up and realized she had been reading what I had written. I handed her a Kleenex.

"Was this your *Grandmother's* ring?"

She nodded, while dabbing at her eyes.

"Were you two *very close*?"

Again, she nodded. Ruth fought through her emotions and said, "At the end of her life, all she would eat were *Ritz Crackers*."

I returned the ring to Ruth. "I definitely feel your Grandmother is with us." I tore off the sheet of paper and handed it to her.

When Ruth got up to leave she said, "I have to find my sister and show her what you wrote. She's not going to believe *Ritz Crackers*." She thanked me for the reading, and headed out to search for her sister.

I had a scheduled a break, so I walked outside the venue. Andi was kind enough to watch my booth. Finding a shady spot, I sat beneath a large tree to process Ruth's read. I don't normally get emotional when I look at the cards, so being overcome had rattled me. During her read, I plunged back in time, to the last few years of my mother's life. It was a period of pain and sorrow, not only for me, but for my brother and his wife, and for my daughter.

On a Saturday morning, I stood next to my phone when its loud ring startled me. The caller I.D. indicated it was Eddy; I knew something was wrong. I hadn't heard from Eddy since I'd told him I couldn't do Mom anymore. A year earlier, she had unleashed another venomous attack on me, and crossed the line with comments about Kent's suicide. This was not the first estrangement or boundary I had had to set with my Mother. Her most recent verbal assault sent me into self-preservation mode.

I hesitantly picked up the phone. Eddy delivered the news that Mother was in the hospital. He and Laney had come for a visit and found Mom behaving strangely. Eddy said she was "out of it" and the doctors didn't know the cause. (It was later determined that Mom hadn't been taking her prescription medications properly, and had gotten additional meds from girlfriends.) I visited her several times while she was in the hospital, and it became apparent she could no longer live alone.

Eddy moved her to an apartment in an assisted living facility she loved. Mom was familiar with the place because it was where my brother had placed my stepdad when he could no longer care for himself. Eddy shouldered the responsibility, and had Power of Attorney for both parents.

He made critical decisions for both Mom and Dad, and having both parents in the same facility made it easier for all involved. Luckily our parents had remained friends, even though they had divorced years earlier.

The assisted living facility was beautiful. Rich textured carpets adorned the large sitting areas used for family visits. The dining area resembled a nice restaurant. It looked good, but I learned it wasn't a place to be if you were unhealthy.

I referred to the facility as The Hostel. A long list of separate fees indicated what The Hostel could do for its inhabitants. One such fee ensured "med techs" would dispense Mom's medications to her at the correct times and in the proper dosages. We hoped to prevent another episode of her over medicating herself. I was shocked to discover how many medications she took. She had given up alcohol years before, but she made no mention of switching to Xanax and other anti-anxiety and anti-depressant meds. The list of pills filled two pages.

Mom returned to her former self once her medications were under control. It did our hearts good to see her mental clarity return. Every weekend I took her to lunch and grocery shopping. We reconnected, and I was surprised when she apologized for her previous attacks.

After a year in her apartment, Mom began forgetting much more. She called me in tears when she couldn't remember where she had hidden the money she had just withdrawn from the bank. I drove thirty minutes to her apartment and when she answered the door, she was a wreck. Her arms trembled as she reached out to hug me. She calmed down once I found the money stashed in her closet.

One Saturday I went to pick her up for our regular lunch and grocery run, but she wasn't dressed, which was odd. She loved our outings, and was always raring to go. I asked why she wasn't dressed, and she said she had trouble getting into her clothes. I had to dress her, and as I did, I knew something was terribly wrong.

After we got the dementia diagnosis, she seemed to decline rapidly. Forgetting how to dress was the first of many things the disease stole from her. It snuck in on tiptoe like a thief, and took what it wanted. The next to go was her mobility. When Mom had first moved into The Hostel, she walked in under her own power, soon she needed a walker, and by June of 2013 she was in a wheelchair.

I called her neurologist. "How could she go from walking one day to needing a wheelchair the next?"

He said, "Some of my patients just 'hit a wall,' regarding their physical abilities. They suddenly can't dress themselves, brush their teeth and hair, get themselves to the bathroom, or walk. The brain doesn't remember how to do these things."

Over the course of two years, the Mom I knew eroded. There were countless instances that showed she was slipping away. Rolled up used tissues dotted the floor like popcorn. She dropped them in mid-stride, with no thought of a trash can. Soda crackers and cookies went from the kitchen to being stored with her underwear, crumbs everywhere. The drawer looked like the bottom of a cookie jar. My mom had always kept a clean house, the messy apartment was the work of someone I didn't know. Dementia claimed a little more of her each day.

The part of her I missed the most was her sense of humor. She had a quick wit and enjoyed a good laugh, but that had vanished. Thank goodness a sense of humor was the legacy left to Eddy and me, from both our parents.

My brother and I battled with the assisted living facility to get my mom into the memory care unit. We were getting daily calls from The Hostel saying Mom was refusing to go to physical therapy, to meals, and to bathe. She stayed in bed all day. For a fee, food was sent to her room, but she would only order a milkshake. I watched her attempting to drink one while flat on her back. I had fears of her choking, and wondered what else was going on when my brother and I weren't with her.

Even though Mom couldn't do anything physically for herself, and multiple fees were added for additional care, The Hostel advised us that her mental capacity didn't warrant her being placed in the dementia unit—even with a dementia diagnosis. (The Hostel made more money from Mom staying in her apartment, being charged a separate fee for every service, than they would had she gone into the all-inclusive memory care unit.) My brother and I were furious.

Shortly after The Hostel told us Mom wouldn't be allowed into the dementia care unit, I received a call. It was late September, at 6:19 a.m. My Mother had fallen again, and The Hostel had put her into an ambulance, headed to Sutter General. This was an opportunity to get her the 24 hour care she needed.

Mom begged the emergency room doctor to send her back to The Hostel, but I spoke to him privately and explained she wasn't receiving the appropriate care. My brother and I insisted she go to a skilled nursing home. To return to The Hostel, the nursing home would have to sign off that Mom was "thriving."

Mother was angry that she wasn't allowed to return to her apartment, but I was grateful she would now get the care she needed and deserved. The skilled nursing facility had nurses on duty 24/7. This gave Eddy and me time to find a facility that specialized in dementia care. A place that put the care of an individual above the need of the almighty dollar.

We learned Mom wasn't eating, and probably hadn't been eating for some time. That hadn't been monitored at The Hostel. The staff at the nursing home were great, and took valiant measures to try to get her to eat, but she wouldn't cooperate. An employee from The Hostel visited her, and brought a huge cupcake with frosting. Everyone knew of Mom's sweet tooth, and that she never missed an opportunity for a treat, but the cupcake went uneaten.

In the midst of all the gloominess, an odd compulsion took hold. I *had* to listen to my first psychic reading with Caroline. I hadn't listened to the CD for a year, but now I listened to it over and over. It unnerved me that I still couldn't identify the spirit who knew "formulaic math," and was "good with numbers." The same spirit who gave Caroline the symbol of a compass. Not a compass used for direction, but the tool that looked like an upside down V, with a point on one leg, and a pencil on the other. (A drawing tool, that could also be used to measure distance.) I was blocked on who this spirit was, and that added to my frustration.

Mom's health woes were never far from my thoughts. I kept being reminded of what had occurred nine months earlier, in January of 2013. My Mother looked me in the eyes and told me she was not going to live to see her next birthday. I asked her not to talk that way. "Why would you say such a thing?"

"I just feel it," Mom said. Now, in the nursing home, she repeated the same premonition. Chills ran down my spine; her birthday was less than thirty days away.

She had always been a strong and vigorous woman, but now it felt like she was giving up. She had no fight left. She had no quality of life, and her days consisted of being confined to a bed. I prayed she would cross over for selfish reasons. Watching her die was ripping my heart out.

During a visit at the skilled nursing facility the Head Nurse took me aside. "Your mom may not last the week."

I called Eddy. He and Laney would drive up on Saturday. I told Mom Eddy and Laney were coming, and prayed she would live long enough to see them.

By Saturday, Mom could no longer speak. Eddy sat next to her bed, wearing sunglasses, to hide the pain in his eyes. She was skeletal and stared into the distance. She appeared to be transfixed on something of great importance, which only she could see. My sister-in-law and I went back to my house to give Eddy some time alone with Mom.

I was glad my daughter was at home when we walked in. Katie hadn't seen her Grandma for some time, and I told her if she wanted to say good-bye, it was time. Katie returned to the nursing home with us.

Katie got up on the bed with her Grandma, and held her hands and told her it was going to be all right. That angels were all around her and that she was loved by us all. That's when Eddy and I lost it.

We stayed for a while, but by 4:00 p.m. we all needed an emotional break. I kissed Mom and told her we would be back later. I squeezed her hand, but got nothing in return. She continued to stare at her special spot with mouth wide open.

Once home, I was *compelled* to find Mom's birth certificate. I went into the extra bedroom closet, and pulled down an Army green metal box. The box held Mom's important papers. Rifling through various documents, my hand landed on a black leather case, the size of a pocket book. I turned it over and engraved in gold was a picture of a compass. Below that was the name "Little Daddy," my Grandfather. Chills swept over me and then I broke down sobbing. This was the spirit who was "good with numbers." I was four when he died, and I had never thought about what he'd done for a living. All the work stories my mom and Grandma had shared flooded back. He'd been a Certified Public Accountant for the State of California, and had travelled up and down the state for his job. It was heartwarming to know that my Grandfather's spirit had tried to come through at the reading with

Caroline, and had been with me for a long time. I could feel him now.

I asked Little Daddy to bring his daughter across. She needed him more than ever. I prayed he would have the rest of the family waiting for her.

While I was lost in thought, the phone jarred me. It was Eddy. He told me that Mom had passed away at 6:25 p.m. It was October 19th, nine days shy of her 77th birthday. She died an hour after I found my Grandfather's black leather case. I knew they were all together, and I was grateful Mom was no longer suffering.

The next morning I met my brother and Laney. We had several matters to discuss. Even though we were all overwrought, I had to tell them the story about my psychic reading and discovering Little Daddy's black leather compass case. I pulled the case from my purse, and handed it to my brother. He inspected it carefully. "I have the compass . . . I used it all through college. Mom gave it to me over 30 years ago. Do you mind if I keep the case?"

It only seemed right that the case and the compass be together with Little Daddy's grandson, his namesake.

A bright point of my mother's life, and her legacy, was the hundreds of lives she touched as an elementary school teacher. She was an excellent teacher, and I followed her into that career. As a child I spent time in her classrooms, and saw the devotion and love that passed between her and her kids. At first I was jealous of their connection, but eventually I grew to admire and respect the relationships she had with her students. Mom devoted twenty-nine years to educating young people. When her students were old enough to have children of their own, she taught some of them.

The elementary school where she taught fed into the junior high I attended. When kids heard my last name, I was asked if I was any relation to her. When I said I was her daughter, they would launch into their special stories. I heard many times how she was their favorite teacher. I learned from others that they hadn't been in her classroom, but they knew her from the playground when she did yard-duty. She would jump into a game of kickball, and would astound them by sending the ball skyward. The adoration was evident on their glowing faces.

I miss my mother more than I thought possible, even though there are scars from how she parented. The woman who gave me life also gave me many loves. My love for reading, education, Disneyland, football, and animals, all came from her. She taught me how to be a good employee, how to make lists and be organized, and how to maintain a house.

I have so many questions about family gatherings, and ancestors. Because Mom was the guardian of our history, there is no one left to ask.

I wish I had questioned her more when there was time, but I was foolish.

I look back on my youth, and see the wonderful birthdays, vacations, and Christmases she made happen. As a parent, I understand the energy, time and effort she put into those special events. My birthday is when I feel her absence the most; I still check the mailbox for a card that never comes.

13

A Bit Out of the Norm

My second appearance at the Healing Arts Festival blessed me with another poignant reading. One that involved mothers and daughters, yet again.

I couldn't wait to pack my vehicle like an overstuffed suitcase, with privacy screens, tables, chairs, tablecloths, tarot cards, and my six foot banner; all the tools of the trade. It was that time of year again.

As the fair and festival season got underway, I was grateful to be busy and to share in so many interesting experiences. Each time a new person sat across from me, it was like opening a beautiful gift. Once unwrapped, it became crystal clear why we had been placed together.

In my experience, customers always took something away from their readings. Sometimes a person may not recognize or understand some of the information, and that could be in part due to my interpretation. I try to explain what I'm receiving in as many ways as I can, but sometimes I'm not successful. Often times the sitter comprehends everything I'm saying. Two such readings pierced my heart, but for different reasons. One was for the unexpected raw emotions shared, and the other for the presence of spirit.

The first reading occurred while at the Turlock Expo. Puffy white clouds dotted a blue sky, and I was thankful for the good weather. After my booth was assembled, I heard the clang of the heavy metal doors being opened to the public. I was ready.

People meandered into the building to check out each colorful booth. As usual, readers were plentiful, so customers had a sizable selection. I was flanked by an animal reader on one side, and a psychic medium on the other.

As I looked to my left, I saw a handsome young man pushing a baby stroller. I glanced around for a woman accompanying him, but didn't see one. Typically, there are not many men at psychic fairs. The few in attendance are usually forced there by a woman, like a cow to slaughter. Maybe men didn't feel comfortable with intuition and readings. They seem to put more stock in what can be observed and touched. So witnessing a lone male with a baby was more than a bit out of the norm.

The man's dark hair was cut short, and he wore jeans and an ink-black short-sleeved T-shirt that stretched tight across his chest. It didn't escape me that he was very fit, with well-defined muscles. He appeared to be in his early thirties. As he paused to read my banner, I said, "Hello."

He greeted me with a bright smile. His attention was diverted when the baby began to fuss. He bent over to touch the child, and spoke soothingly. When quiet was restored, he stood and made his way up the aisle, away from me.

More people made their way in, and I welcomed each one as they stopped to ask about my readings or just passed by. Out of the corner of my eye, I saw the young dad again. He stopped a few feet away, took another look at my banner and then at me.

"Would you like to get a reading?"

"I think . . . I would," he said, and moved closer to the table. We introduced ourselves, and I learned his name was Jamie.

I invited him back to my sanctuary, and told him to bring his child, which I could clearly see was a boy. I could tell the young dad was nervous.

"Have you ever had a tarot reading before?"

"No, I've never been to anything like this." Jamie nodded his head, indicating the room.

"I get a lot of first timers," I said, trying to put him at ease. "It's easy. I'm going to ask you to pick some cards that I believe your soul wishes to discuss. I'll talk about the cards, and if what I'm saying makes no sense to you, then please let me know. If what I'm saying resonates with you, then it's okay to speak up at any time. Other information may come to me while you are sharing. My readings are two-way streets. Are you ready to begin?"

"Yes," he said. He glanced over to check on his son, who was sleeping peacefully.

I shuffled and fanned the cards across the purple tablecloth. Jamie's eyes moved back and forth across the table as he methodically made his selections.

While eyeing the top three cards of the spread, a heaviness came over me. I heard, *He's gone through so much.* The three cards felt tied together, as if bound by a thick rope. They were: Mental Conflict, Moving On, and Deception & Envy.

I looked up at him and began. "My head is swimming and I feel a bit dizzy from too much thought. This is what your mind feels like to me. You are beating yourself up, mentally, with rapid-fire thoughts, like a jack hammer to concrete. This is what I sense from the Mental Conflict card.

You are spending way too much time in your head, obsessing about something. Do you know what this is?"

"Yes," Jamie said, his eyes wide.

I continued. "The Deception & Envy card speaks of something going on at a person's work, like a petty grievance or a personality conflict. Where hidden agendas may be coming to light, or you're aware that someone is envious of your abilities. The card also warns of having a 'Plan B' regarding some effort you may be trying to put forth."

I took a sip of water, then turned the Moving On card towards him and said, "This card tells me there is a situation in your life that no longer serves you, that you need to move on from it. Or it could be a person you need to step away from. I feel the three cards are bound together around a certain situation in you life. Can you tell me what's been going on?"

Jamie ran his fingers through his hair. "I work for a large construction company, and I injured my back six months ago and went on Workers' Compensation. Surgery was necessary and I've been struggling to recover." He bowed his head for a few minutes.

My thoughts raced to my husband's back injury, and his eventual downfall. I felt compassion for the young man before me.

Jamie raised his head. "Just before the injury, I was promoted and I was on top of the world, so happy and proud. I had a friendship with the boss who had promoted me, but now he won't even talk to me, or return my phone calls. I heard through the rumor-mill that he resented my going on Workers' Comp." Without warning tears cascaded down Jamie's cheeks; he quickly wiped them away. In a choked voice he said, "This is so embarrassing. I don't know why I'm doing this."

"Don't worry about the tears, it happens all the time," I said. I produced a box of Kleenex. He waived away the box, and continued to use his hands to dry his face. I returned the Kleenex to their secret spot on the floor behind the folds of the tablecloth.

"I'm so confused," Jamie said. "I'm cleared to return to work next week, and I just learned I've been transferred to another division. I don't even know if I should physically do the work anymore. On top of that, I lost my promotion. I feel so betrayed." He apologized again for crying.

"Please don't bother about the tears. It appears you needed to let your feelings out. It's an honor when people feel safe enough to cry. Are you on any pain medications?"

"No."

I was relieved. "You said you weren't sure if you should physically do the work anymore. Are you trained for other types of employment?"

"I got my real estate license, just in case," Jamie said. "I have a family to support. I've invested twelve years with the construction company, and it pays well, but I'm so torn about what I should do."

"You have had so much physically and emotionally going on, who are you sharing your pain with?"

"At first, just my wife, but I know the situation stresses her out. So I've been keeping things to myself."

"Counseling has been a lifesaver for me. I believe there are times in our lives when we need a professional, an outside party, who will listen to us and maybe offer solutions we could never see on our own. Have you done any counseling?"

"I had an appointment a few months back, but I never showed up. I thought I didn't need it, but after today, I'm rethinking that one," he said, with a bit of a grin.

During a read, I am often compelled to talk about certain things; this one was no different. We spent time exploring various work options, and tossed around the idea of him starting up the real estate on weekends. I assured him it wasn't necessary to figure out his whole life today. He should give himself time to assess how he felt, after he returned to work. He would have more information then to make better decisions.

Jamie still had two more cards in his spread. The meaning of one had already come out during our discussion; this happens often. He had selected the Firm Foundation card, which shows the back of a muscled black man standing before a mountain. On his lower back is a large red triangle. This card speaks to me of two things. The sitter has a solid and supportive home life. It also may say the sitter has back pain or an injury of some kind, or someone close to them does. Not surprising this card was part of his read.

I held up his last card. "The Hope card is the most important card for you today. It's about having faith and trust that all will work out. I feel it's a reminder for you to reach out to whoever your higher power may be, and ask for help. We don't have to carry our burdens alone, and when they get to be too much, we can turn them over to a power greater than ourselves. This card is about healing, and I feel you are on your way."

He gave a smile and a silent nod.

We had gone over our time. I thanked him for being courageous and for spending time with me.

Jamie leaned forward as if he had a secret. "You know, I walked around this entire room, and checked out all the readers, but something brought me back here. It feels like it was meant to be, that I was *supposed* to get a reading from you today."

"That's how it works," I said, and stood to give him a hug. There was a lighter air about him as he gazed at his still sleeping son. He took hold of the stroller and eased his way out of the venue.

The second read that created a lasting impression happened in Sacramento, while at the Healing Arts Festival. I was booked with back-to-back readings, and my friend Andi was assisting me. As I said goodbye to one customer, Andi introduced me to the next, Elizabeth.

I guessed she was in her late 20s to early 30s. She was of average build and height. What stood out was her two-toned hair. The top layer was a vivid pink, like a Valentine heart, and the blonde bottom layer fell just past her shoulders. Her pierced nose sported a tiny diamond that sparkled when the light caught it.

As we took our seats, Elizabeth said, "I have to tell you, I researched all the readers here, and I read your bio on the Healing Arts website. Besides the tarot, it said you also do psychometry. So I brought something for you to hold today."

"Well, this is a first. I've never had anyone bring something special, or who has taken the time to read my biography. People are unaware that I do psychometry, so I just hold whatever objects they have on them at the time, like rings, necklaces, keys, or sunglasses."

Elizabeth asked, "Do you want to hold the item now?"

"No, I'd rather begin with the tarot and do a soul read first. It's a way for me to ground in. I'll make sure to allow more time for the psychometry."

I explained how I worked, and that she was welcome at any time to let me know if something didn't make sense or when something felt on-point.

The first card Elizabeth drew was Heartache & Loss. The card was bordered in blue, and the artwork showed a woman with long auburn hair, standing head bowed. She wore a necklace, and a red heart appliqué was sewn into the center of her dark mermaid gown. The woman's palms were pressed together, held low over her abdomen.

"This card usually means there is someone who has passed from your life, or there's a relationship lost. Who would this be?"

"That would be my girlfriend, Stacey. She died almost a year ago." Elizabeth grabbed a strand of her blonde hair, and twisted it between her fingers. She looked uneasy. "If you don't mind, I really don't want to talk about her right now."

"That's fine by me. You don't need to say a word."

The rest of the read focused on Elizabeth's employment. The cards showed she was at a crossroad where her work was concerned. We brainstormed options that might be of help. She felt stuck at work and wanted to move on.

When her tarot read was over, we got to the main reason for her appointment. Elizabeth gently pulled an object from her purse. It was wrapped in a large white scarf. She unfolded the silky material to reveal a 4 X 4 inch tile. I could tell the tile had been painted and fired by a child. I felt like I wasn't supposed to examine the tile closely.

I asked Elizabeth to place the tile in my palm, and closed my eyes. I silently asked my angels and guides to allow me to receive images or messages that would be helpful to Elizabeth.

Spirit gets me to say certain words by giving me images from my own data bank. The image of a child's *swing* drifted onto my internal screen. It was a swing I had enjoyed as a kid. There were two swings and supporting each were the longest chains imaginable. The chains hung from a heavy metal frame. The length of the swing meant it could go higher than normal. I used to lean back and pump my legs, and get so high I could almost take a bite out of a cloud. Today these contraptions would be deemed too dangerous. I thanked my guides for the image and wrote *swing* down on my tablet.

Next I felt like I was at the top of a *log ride* at an *amusement park*. I was filled with excitement, poised in the moment before the log takes the stomach-turning plunge into the waters below.

Other items that dropped in were *cotton candy* and *red-whip licorice*. Then a troubling thing occurred. While attempting to open up to receive more items, a distinct image emerged in the space between my brows. Normally I get a one dimensional picture, but this image felt *alive*. I'm sure I looked my usual self on the outside, but on the inside, I panicked. *What the hell was going on? Why was this coming in now?*

I concentrated. A black and white silhouette picture of a woman appeared, from the chest up. Light radiated from behind her head, illuminating individual wisps of her hair. Her face had no features; it was a dark blank canvas. The image exuded warmth. There was a glow coming from her chest. Where pearls might hang, was a fluorescent V-shape about two inches in width. The necklace of light that adorned her neck was vibrant.

Elizabeth had no idea of the mental battle that waged within my head, or the uniqueness of the vision. My eyes popped open. "Did your girlfriend that died wear a special necklace?"

Elizabeth smiled. She lifted the necklace she wore around her neck. It was light brown, and the strand held wooden beads and hearts in various sizes. "This is my necklace, but my girlfriend always wore it." Tears welled up in her eyes. "I asked my girlfriend to either make you comment on this ring," holding up a hand to me, "or to have you comment on the necklace."

I didn't know what to say, I was so touched by the experience. I returned the tile to Elizabeth.

In a hushed tone I said, "I'd like to give you the other images and feelings I received while I held the tile." I read my list; "*Swing, amusement park, cotton candy* and *red-whip licorice.*" I related the detailed impressions that went with the words. Elizabeth nodded her head while I spoke.

"They all make sense to me," she said. "My girlfriend and I were friends since the second grade. We had countless sleep-overs and trips together, and we loved amusement parks. We went on the scariest rides, and ate cotton candy and red-whip licorice until we were sick."

I said, "From the images I get the feeling that your girlfriend wants you to focus on all the positive and fun-filled adventures you two had. To be grateful for the time you were given."

"I'm getting that also," Elizabeth said.

"What about the swing?" I asked, curious about that vision.

A grin lit up Elizabeth's face. "Two days ago I was at a park that had swings, and something compelled me to get on one. It had been years. At first, I was flapping around like an injured pelican, trying to propel myself skyward. I finally got my rhythm, but the silliness of the situation made me think of my girlfriend, and our crazy escapades. The entire time I moved through the air, I spoke to her."

Just then, another image was given. "I'm being shown you weren't alone while you were swinging, Stacey was by your side, joyfully matching your every swing."

14

A Theme Runs Through It

I've noticed while working the fairs and festivals that a theme runs through the reads. Certain cards are picked over and over again. The Heartache & Loss card is a good example. The theme will be the loss of a loved one, followed by a discussion of grief. Work is another theme, as is self-confidence. The venues may change, but a "like" vibration runs through the people attending.

At a recent event, marriages and relationships were the theme. The overriding question from the sitters was "Should I stay, or should I go?" The topic didn't present itself by the picking of one particular card; various cards led to the same issue.

As I've mentioned earlier in this book, people sit across from me who are often in situations I've experienced. I wasn't surprised that unhappy marriages was a theme, since I'd been married three times. I understand what it means to be at a crossroads, to fall out of love with a partner, and to choose divorce. The tarot might show a person whether one direction is more favorable than another. The cards might also provide different insights to the sitter; ones the sitter hadn't considered. Ultimately, I believe whether a person stays in a relationship, or leaves it, is a decision only the individual can make.

During a read I'm compelled to talk about certain points. My hope is that I'm used as a vessel, and that helpful information will come through me for the person getting the reading. This was the case for two women who sat at my table. One listened while the other had the reading, and then they switched seats.

Linda plunked down into the chair across from me. She selected the Shadow card. It showed two men in robes facing each other, each with a hand on an ornate gold staff held between them. On closer inspection, it becomes clear it's the same man standing across from himself. One man was in light due to the sun above his head. A silhouette of the sun shown on his robe. The other man was in dim light due to the moon above his head. A silhouette of the moon was on his robe.

I explained to Linda that the card was about facing her fears. There was something specific she'd been thinking, troubling in nature, and it was time to deal with it. "Do you understand this card?"

"Yes," Linda said, as she ran her fingers through shoulder-length grey hair. "I know what it's about. It's my marriage. I don't know what to do; I've been on the fence. I've been thinking about leaving, but I'm afraid. Afraid to stay and afraid to go."

"I understand your dilemma because I've been married a few times myself. I want to ask, are you past the point of no return? For me that is when you are no longer in love with your partner, and no amount of counseling can repair the damage."

Linda hesitated. "I don't know if I'm there yet. I've been with my husband for over forty years, and we have so much history. He's an alcoholic." Linda paused, and inhaled deeply. "If he, or we got help, it might make a difference, but he won't go to counseling."

"I've been in a similar situation." I shared some of my own marriage history with Linda. I told her it only took one person changing to shake up the stagnant energy in a relationship. I went to counseling on my own, and to Al-Anon.

I encouraged her to find something that worked for her, some place where she might find relief.

"I sense I'm supposed to throw this idea out to you. Have you thought about falling in love with your husband all over again? Think about what drew you to him originally. What do you love about him? Sometimes just changing the focus, and looking at his positive traits can bring in a renewed energy."

Linda's eyes opened wide. "I've never thought to fall in love again."

"You may also want to compliment your husband, or let him know when he does something you appreciate. I know when I was unhappy, I would shutdown and I stopped communicating. It may not hurt to try some of these ideas. You will certainly know if they work or not."

Linda nodded. "I know I've been shutdown, and haven't been talking much lately. You've given me some things to consider."

Linda's friend, Vanna, sat like a statue in the chair next to me during her friend's read. When I finished with Linda, they both stood and traded places. Vanna had already heard and seen how I worked, so we got underway.

The first card I wanted to talk to Vanna about was the Emotional Withdrawal card. Bordered in green, it showed a man sitting on a beach in quiet reflection. His back to us, he wore a robe draped over one shoulder, and his palms were pressed together in prayer.

"This card presents itself when a person should step away from a certain situation. When something no longer serves you, and you need to take a break. Does this make sense?"

"It does. My marriage is not good, and my husband is also an alcoholic. I can tell you, I am way past the point of no return."

"Can you financially afford to leave?"

"No, I can't." Vanna looked at Linda, and then back at me. "We have been living in separate bedrooms for some time now."

"I know how difficult that can be. I did it for a time myself. I know you've already heard me talk about counseling and Al-Anon as healthy tools to explore. They may also be beneficial to you. When a relationship gets to the point of separate bedrooms, I believe in making it as peaceful, tolerable, and respectful as possible."

"It's none of those things right now," Vanna said.

"Well, you also drew the Hope card. This is about your spirituality and faith. It feels that this is an element for you to rely on, given the situation."

"I have been working on my faith, and it is helping. That's one thing I feel good about."

"When things got rough for me, it was important to keep the focus on myself. I needed to do healthy and fun things that helped me stay in a positive frame of mind. You might find this helpful as well. Another thing that comes to mind is making your bedroom a sanctuary, if you haven't done so already. Fill it with things you love. You may even wish to create a small altar."

Vanna chuckled. "My room is a disaster, and I haven't given it any thought. I like the idea of fixing it up, and having it become a sanctuary."

When it was time for them to leave, both women told me they had gotten something from their readings. Each gave me a hug as they exited the booth.

I read a few more women, and then a gentleman stepped up to my table. We introduced ourselves, and I learned his name was David. He was a short stocky man, and looked to be in his early fifties. His hair was dark, and he sported a tan. I noticed a serious look on his face as he sat down. He locked his arms across his chest. Never a good sign.

"Have you ever had a reading before?"

"Yes, many."

I said a hasty silent prayer. I shuffled the cards, and spread them out before him. David made fast work of the cards. He, too, selected the Hope card.

"This is about spirituality," I said, as I turned the card toward him. "Do you have a higher power in your life? It might be Source, Jesus, Buddha, but do you have something?"

"I was raised Catholic, but I don't buy into all that nonsense."

I tried again. "Do you believe in a power greater than yourself?"

David scrunched up his face, and shifted in his chair. It was clear he was not used to questions like this. "I believe there is a power greater than me," he said grudgingly. "I'll call it Universe."

"How is your relationship with your higher power?"

"What do you mean by that?"

"I mean, do you feel connected? Do you have a working relationship with the Universe? Do you pray? When you are troubled, do you ask for assistance, and turn your worries over to your higher power?"

He stared at me, and took some time to respond. "I don't really have a relationship with my higher power presently."

"When this card is selected, it's about your soul wanting you to take a look at the situation. You may want to consider improving that relationship."

I turned the Disruption card toward him. It showed a man standing with his arms locked across his chest, hands clenched into fists. His body was sectioned off into disjointed boxes, as if he were coming apart. In the Rider-Waite deck it's the Tower Card. It means a relationship or a situation is unraveling. The relationship or belief had not been built on firm-footing, and it needed to be rebuilt.

"This card appears when something is crumbling, or falling apart. Is something in your life unraveling?"

David began to speak, but stopped. I could see the confusion on his face, as his eyes filled with tears. I knew he was not in the habit of crying, especially in front of a stranger.

I looked at him and said, "I know . . . I know."

He took a few minutes to gather himself. "It's my marriage. I don't know whether I should stay, or I should go. I'm just so lost."

I shared with David that I believed his marriage woes were a karmic lesson. That no one could make the decision for him. His internal struggle to a resolution would provide growth and expansion of his soul.

"It's no accident that you selected the Hope card. Your relationship is something you may wish to pray about, or that you surrender to your higher power. By doing so, a relationship with Universe may develop, and you won't have to carry your burdens alone. I know improving my connection to God helped a great deal."

"I'll give it some thought," David said.

My timer had gone off, so I finished with his cards. He thanked me for the reading, and wanted to know if I was local. I gave him my business card, and he said there were other family members who might like a reading. That surprised me because I wasn't sure if he took the reading to heart.

The next person sat down at my table. I explained how I worked, and she picked her cards. Within short order, she revealed she wanted out of her marriage. She had already left it and come back to it a few times.

I said, "What is in the air today?" The woman looked at me quizzically. "You are the fifth person today with marriage as an issue."

"You're joking."

"I wish I were."

I believe in love and doing whatever one can to save a relationship. Each of my marriages began with the hope that it would last, and we would grow old together. I've learned that people and circumstances can change. Being in an unhappy and unhealthy relationship was exhausting. Making the decision to leave filled my heart with sadness. I empathized with the sitters, since I'd chosen divorce twice. The decision was never made lightly.

I had made a vow to *not* stay in a marriage that was abusive, or one that no longer worked.

We humans are meant to be happy and joyous. It's my job to create a lifestyle where those feelings exist and are nurtured. I watched my parents stay in their relationship long past the expiration-date, making everyone miserable. I swore I wouldn't do that to myself, or to any children I might have.

My heart goes out to those I read, and anyone struggling with the "stay or go" dilemma. Living through a divorce is life-changing, and it takes inner strength to start over. The experience grows our souls in ways we may not be aware of until much later. Having faith, and taking one day at a time, made my journey easier. Healing from one bad relationship eventually led to another lesson in love.

15

My Own Lesson of Free Will

ree will was a topic that often popped up in readings. When sitters asked questions about the future, I'd have to explain that tarot cards were about probabilities, the likelihood of something occurring, nothing was cast in stone. Making choices has the power to affect our lives, either positively or negatively. Like the person who booked passage on the last voyage of the Titanic, or Princess Diana choosing to leave a hotel room late at night with her boyfriend. Some moments of free will cost dearly, while others bring great joy.

Some choices may have no consequence at all, while others may push a desperate desire even further away. We might be oblivious to the consequences until the lesson is learned in hindsight. That's how my own lesson of free will came to light.

It was the last quarter of 1989. I had met a new friend, Jan, and while visiting she let it slip she had plans to get a reading with a psychic. I tried to keep the shock off my face but failed. Seeing my stunned look, Jan admitted to having had several readings. At the time, no one in my circle spoke of such things, let alone did them.

Jan couldn't contain her excitement. She spoke so rapidly, I had a hard time following. I did catch that a psychic could see into the future. My friend divulged that she had also taken some classes at a nearby psychic institute. I didn't know there was such a thing. Jan surprised me when she asked if I wanted to sign-up for a reading. I was scared, but figured if my mild-mannered friend could do it, so could I.

The day of reckoning came. Mary, the reader, was doing readings out of a friend's home, which seemed strange until I learned she didn't live in Sacramento.

I sat uncomfortably in a living room decorated in various shades of gold. Fidgeting, I twisted some of my newly permed brown hair around my index finger. Some said I looked a bit like Bette Midler in her movie "The Rose," but I didn't think so.

When I arrived at the house, Lauri answered the door and stated that someone was with Mary, and it wouldn't be too long for my turn. I waited alone on a honey-colored sofa, wondering how Jan's reading had gone. Her appointment had been at 10:00 a.m. and mine was set for 1:00 p.m., so we hadn't driven together.

I heard a door open and people mumbling, making their way up a hall. Two women appeared, both said hello. I wondered which was Mary, when one woman said, "I'll be on my way, and thanks again."

Mary turned to me. "You must be my one o'clock."

I nodded and stood. I held out my hand. "I'm Erin."

Mary was older, perhaps in her sixties. She was plump, and wore a faded floral shift. Her hair was wavy and grey, and fell to just above her shoulders. Steel-rimmed glasses, pointed at the corners, adorned her face. She radiated calm, and she gave me a sweet smile.

She beckoned me to follow, and led me down a hallway into a back bedroom. She sat in a rocker and I took the chair across from her. I noticed a black cassette recorder on a small ornate wood table next to her. She saw my glance and told me she would record the session, and I could keep the tape.

"Have you ever had a reading?" Mary asked.

"No," I said. "My girlfriend, that you saw at 10:00 a.m., told me she gets them all the time. I was curious, so here I am."

"I'm glad you are here. You can ask any questions you'd like, and I'll see what information comes to me. Are you ready to get started?"

Not trusting my memory, I pulled a list of questions from my purse. "I am now."

Mary pushed the "record" button on the cassette player and said, "What is it you would like to know?"

I glanced at my list. "Do you see me getting a promotion at work anytime soon?" I had taken a cut in pay to get my foot in the door with the State, and was in need of more money.

She hesitated for an instant, cocking her head to tune into something I couldn't see. "I do see you getting a promotion, but it will be at least six months before it happens." I'm sure the disappointment showed on my face.

Mary said, "I feel there are certain things that have to fall into place with higher-ups for this promotion to happen. That's why I get extra time is needed."

I asked many questions during my time with Mary, but I saved the most important one for last. "I've been single for some time now, and feel ready to meet someone special. Do you see me in a loving relationship?"

She grinned. "I get asked that question a lot."

"I bet you do."

Mary squinted her eyes and said, "Around the first of the year, I see a gentleman coming into your life. You are going to really enjoy this person. The relationship will feel very different from others you've had."

"Hallelujah!" I interrupted, and we both laughed.

Mary's expression changed and she grew thoughtful. "This man will be very deep and serious, you will be able to talk to him at length. He has a lot of patience, but when he is done with a person or situation, he's *done*. There will be no changing his mind once he's decided to let go or end something."

"Interesting," I said. I was very curious about this man. I did want to share my life with someone, and looked forward to meeting this mystery man. Mary's next words brought me back from my musings.

"I'm sorry, we've run out of time." She stopped the recorder and ejected the cassette, handing it to me. She said I could contact Jan if I ever wanted another reading.

The hour had sped by, and I was glad for the experience; it was much different from my normal Saturday activities.

In the days and weeks that followed, I listened to my tape many times. Hoping what Mary had said about the unknown man would come to pass.

On New Year's Eve, I met some friends at an open Alcoholics Anonymous meeting. Nonmembers like me, an Al Anon member, were welcome on holidays. Meetings went all night to give people in recovery a safe place to go, especially tonight, the busiest drinking night of the year. After the hour meeting, an acquaintance named Sam invited me to coffee. I didn't have any other plans, so I agreed to go.

I drove my own car and met him at a Denny's. We ordered coffee and chatted politely, getting to know one another. We were both divorced, he had a young son. Sam and I each shared our story of how we found our way into recovery, me to Al Anon, him to AA. We also discovered we had a couple of mutual friends.

Our time together was pleasant enough, a couple of hours had passed, but my rear end had gone to sleep. I told Sam it was time for me to go.

He walked me to my car and looked down at his feet, kicking unseen pebbles. "Would you like to come back to my apartment?"

I was surprised by the invite. Sam was a nice guy, funny, and not bad looking, but I wasn't attracted to him. As some say, he didn't float my boat. I wouldn't mind talking to him some more and going to his place, but I wasn't up for the "just friends" conversation.

"No thanks. I'll just be heading home." I was glad to see that he took it well.

"Happy New Year," he said with a wave.

The New Year came and went, and there was still no sign of Prince Charming. I had been keeping a watchful eye out for him and his horse, but nothing galloped by. Disappointed, I booked another psychic reading.

In early April of 1990, I sat before Mary once again. I wanted only one thing from my reading. I said, "The last time I was here, you said you saw me getting into a relationship at the first of the year. Well, the first of the year has come and gone, so I'm wondering if you still see me with this person?"

Mary nodded. "I do still see it happening, but you need to be aware that you can make choices that change the timing of an event. You may get an invite to a party and decide not to go, and that's where the meeting was to occur. Please be aware that a free will decision can move something further out. I still see him, and it will happen this year."

I'd never considered free will and how my choices might modify an outcome. It was food for thought, and I chewed on it like a tough steak.

I went about my normal life. To help in my search for my next love, I told all my friends I was ready to date again, but my phone remained silent.

Then one day I received a call from Andrew. He was a friend I'd met in recovery. He sounded a bit embarrassed, as he told me there was a man he'd met that he thought I might like. I gave Andrew the go-ahead to pass on my phone number.

I waited through a nerve-wracking week, but no call came. I checked my phone several times to see if it was still working, it was. I phoned Andrew and asked what was up. He said he had no idea. I wasn't bashful. I asked Andrew to ask his friend if I could have his number because I would make the call.

Andrew got back to me within an hour, with the number. His buddy hadn't worked up the courage to call a woman he didn't know. I'd take care of that. I managed to wait a day before I placed the call. Once past the awkwardness, we made a date to meet for coffee in two days time. During our conversation, I learned he lived not far from me, and that I jogged by his apartment complex every other day. Since I planned to head out for a run, I asked if I could swing by his place to meet him, so we could avoid the whole blind date thing when we met for coffee. He agreed.

I started my jog; the running helped calm my anxiety somewhat, but didn't help with my racing mind. With each stride another thought sprinted into my head. Is he the one? Will we get along? Will I like his looks?

It was a blessing it didn't take long to reach my destination. I took a few deep breaths and knocked. I could hear footsteps, and as the door swung open, I was overcome. He was . . . gorgeous. My boat was now floating skyward.

His black hair swept across his forehead, and I could see a hint of grey at the temples. He had large brown eyes that boasted lashes any woman would have killed for. A mustache rested below a straight nose, and a light stubble grew along his jawline. He was dressed in a tank top and running shorts, and it was clear he took care of himself. The first thought that registered was, *You are way out of your league, girlfriend.*

He smiled warmly, exposing perfect white teeth. He extended a hand and said, "Hi, I'm Kent."

I managed to collect enough of my wits, and reached out and grasped his hand. "Hello, I'm Erin." Electric pulses shot up my arm, enhancing my already firm grip. I didn't want to let go, but good manners prevailed.

He invited me to come in, but I was too overwhelmed. I said, "I want to continue on my jog. I just wanted to meet you so I would know who to look for at coffee. I'm sure you have things to do."

"Well," Kent said, "then I'll see you on Monday. It was nice to meet you."

"Looking forward to it." I smiled and waved goodbye.

Thank goodness I was on a run. I needed to burn off the rush of adrenaline that was surging through my body. I'd never experienced a reaction like that to anyone. Excitement quickly gave way to disappointment. By the time I got home, I'd convinced myself that Kent wouldn't find me attractive. I had it over before it had begun.

I expected to get a call from Kent cancelling our coffee date, but none came. I showed up at our agreed upon time and place. I scanned the room looking for "my hunk of burning love," but he was nowhere in sight. Maybe he wasn't going to show.

A tap on my shoulder startled me.

"I didn't mean to scare you, " Kent said.

"That's all right."

"How about you find us a table," Kent said, while looking around the room, "and I'll get our coffees. What would you like?"

I gave him my order and went in search of a table. I waved to him, and he made his way across the room with our drinks. He took the seat across from me and I loved the view. I asked how he'd found his way to AA and he shared some of his story. We had a lot in common. We had both come from alcoholic homes, and were both choosing to live sober lives. I was relieved to learn he had a sense of humor. It was far too easy and comfortable talking to this man I'd just met. Time evaporated, and several hours passed.

"I think it's funny we live so close to each other. How long have you lived there?"

Kent told me the story of how he had come to live at the apartments, and how he had met his roommate, Sam, another single dad.

"Wait a second," I said. "Your roommate is Sam? Is it Sam Taylor?"

"Yes. Do you know him?"

"I had coffee with him on New Year's Eve. He invited me to come back to his apartment, but I declined."

Kent laughed. "If you had come over, I would have met you then. I was at home with my kids."

Like a slap across my face, the psychic's words came to me. Mary had advised me that I might have made a decision that pushed the meeting of the man she saw further out. I had had my reasons, but declining Sam's invitation prevented me from meeting Kent "around the first of the year." Telling my friends I was ready to date brought an introduction. I saw how my actions and choices might alter events.

I shared this lesson of free will with others in the following years, and in tarot readings many times over.

Tired of sitting, but not wanting our time together to end, Kent and I left the coffee house and walked to a nearby park. I did all the things they say never to do on a first date, like reveal too much about yourself and speak of past relationships. I asked Kent if he was interested in having a relationship, or was he just inclined to date? What did he want a relationship to look like? He answered sincerely, but later revealed my questions had scared the shit out of him.

By the time Kent walked me back to my car, I was certain we would be together. It had nothing to do with the psychic's prediction. While with him a knowingness had come over me. That night I entered into my journal that Kent and I would be a couple, he just didn't realize it yet. I also wrote of free will.

On July 14, the year anniversary of our first coffee date, I gave him a gift. It was an envelope, and nestled within was a copy of my journal entry.

We married two years later, and he loved me in a way no other man had.

16

A Work In Progress

When I began to explore my intuitive abilities, I naively thought that blaring trumpets would precede any incoming messages or images. Thus alerted, I'd know something of import was about to enter my consciousness. That never happened. What came, came unannounced. The words floated in like whispers, soft and gentle, and easily missed. The symbols and images drifted in amidst the debris of many other thoughts. Once I was aware of their subtle nature, it got easier to recognize and latch onto them. Meditating and tarot readings provided the quiet and the practice needed to receive them.

I'm grateful to all who put their trust in me to get a reading. Those beautiful connections furnished the inspiration for this book. I found myself sharing my own story with those who sat across from me. My stories seemed to benefit us both. It was as if I had gone through my own trials, not only for my own growth, but to provide comfort to others.

Writing my story was a risk. I believe in taking healthy risks. When I get out of my comfort zone, I feel both exhilarated and frightened. I feel alive. These same emotions coursed through me when I did presentations at the Healing Arts Festival. Public speaking terrified me, but I did it. I spoke about taking healthy risks, about grief, and about the ways spirit gets our attention, and sends us messages.

My tarot journey has not been without consequences. Along the way, I have lost people I thought were friends. One example occurred years ago. I had lunch with a girlfriend who was a long-time family friend. We were catching up on each other's lives since our last visit. She asked what I'd been up to, and I told her about doing tarot readings for the public. My friend abruptly shut down the conversation by stating that her religion believed tarot card reading was the work of the devil. I was politely asked to not speak of my activities again.

We struggled through the remainder of our lunch. We have not seen or spoken to each other since.

What's next for me? I have no idea. I had no inkling I'd be a widow, learn the tarot, or write. I will continue to go where my gut and intuition lead. I'm in the habit of paying attention to everyday conversations because I believe God and our guides speak through people. I pay particular attention when something resonates in a positive way. It may take awhile to process; I may even say no at first, but I often sense when it's a step I'm supposed to take. For example, when Dänna Wilberg heard I had started a memoir, she invited me to a writer's group. I declined her invitation. After a while, I sensed the invitation was offered for a reason. As for coincidence, I believe there's no such thing. So I went to the writer's group, and have been a member since November of 2016.

I've been humbled by the writing experience, and in awe of the talented writers I've come to know. The writing process has been similar to learning the tarot, in that I've received downloads and felt compelled to write about certain topics. I've met new friends, and grown in unexpected ways. Reliving certain aspects of my life revealed new insights; another layer of the onion peeled. I hope my stories touch others, as I've been touched by the stories told to me.

If as you read this you feel stuck in your life, may you be inspired to do something different, or try something new. May you get quiet, try counseling, get brutally honest, or experience a reading. Whatever it might be, may it shift your focus, and bring movement and wonder.

One lesson I continue to work on is honoring myself. This shows up in many forms. I must honor my intuition and the messages that I receive. I've had to learn to take care of myself. I used to be exhausted from doing too much and from lack of sleep. I had to honor my body by getting eight hours of sleep, exercising, meditating, and eating nutritious food. I had to learn the word "No." My body carries my soul, so it's important to take care of it. I strive to honor Erin, the personality I chose to be in this lifetime.

Though I am sixty, my journey is still unfolding. I am a work in progress. I'm open to, and hope for an opportunity for another great love. I pray I get many more years to evolve, to do readings, and to receive spirit messages. Who knows? There may be another destiny point just around the corner that will send me in a new direction.

I pray that your journey will be as exciting and fulfilling as mine.

Glossary

afterlife: The state of existence after the death of our physical bodies.

aura: A subtle energy field that emanates from everything and everyone.

chakra: According to Yoga philosophy, there are seven main energy centers (chakras) in the human body. They are important to our spiritual and physical well-being.

clairaudience: The intuitive ability to receive information by hearing it (clear hearing) within the mind or from outside.

"clairs": A nickname for combined abilities of clairaudience, claircognizance, clairsentience, and clairvoyance.

claircognizance: The intuitive ability to receive information by knowing it (clear knowing) within the mind.

clairsentience: The intuitive ability to receive information by feeling it (clear feeling) within the body.

clairvoyance: The intuitive ability to receive information by seeing signs and symbols (clear seeing) within the mind.

database: Images, symbols, memories, and signs that have clear personal meanings for you. This database helps to interpret messages from spirit.

de-wheel: The act of taking a friend's or relative's parked car so they can't drive drunk or under the influence. To prevent a drunk driving ticket.

doppelgänger: A double of a living person, or an apparition.

empathic: The ability to sense the emotions of others.

intuition: The ability to receive information from apparently nowhere in the form of a hunch, rather than known facts.

karmic lesson: Something you are meant to learn in this lifetime due to an experience that happened in another lifetime or due to agreements you made prior to being born.

psychic: The ability to receive, access, and transmit information from an individual's aura or from items that belong to the person being read. A psychic may not possess the abilities of a medium.

psychic medium: A psychic person who connects with and passes on information from our loved ones who have died.

psychometry: The ability to receive information about a person or event by holding an inanimate object.

runner: A drinking binge that lasts for days. The individual leaves home and has no contact with family. May last a week or more.

Source: An alternative name for God, Spirit, Universe, Creator, higher power.

soul: The spiritual or immaterial part of a human being or animal; pure consciousness. Also called spirit.

spirit: A person that no longer has a body.

spirit guide: A being who assists us with our spiritual growth through significant life events by guiding and inspiring us.

Acknowledgments

The author would like to give enormous thanks to . . .

The El Dorado Writers Guild. For your warmth, encouragement, and guidance. Always a safe place to grow and experiment.

My Beta readers. For all your comments, corrections, and heartfelt support.

Clients and customers who provided the inspiration for this book.

The Journey Center, and to all of the wonderful healing practitioners that share the space.

Julie, my recovery sister, who was the recipient of my first tarot reading. Bless you.

Carol R. for your teachings, and for keeping the light burning.

Karen for your patience and creative abilities. You gave me the first concrete vision of my book, and my heart soared.

Prasanna for saying yes, and allowing me to be part of her world, The Healing Arts Festival.

Kirk for your generous spirit, and willingness to edit my story. (I must owe you a case of red pens.) My book would not have happened without you. I'm deeply grateful.

Dänna W. for your friendship, having me on your Paranormal Connection TV show, and for opening doors. Your talents are amazing.

Meghan for sharing your love of writing with me, and for a fun tarot weekend.

Al-Anon and the people who "keep coming back." Thanks for showing me the tools and the way.

My girlfriends throughout the years, who answered the calls, and cheered me on.

Heidi and Elena my work family and friends. For listening to my dreams and tales, and staying in touch.

Joan for being my wing-woman at the fairs, and your endless positivity regarding my latest endeavors.

Lauri for being my cake-sister, and for understanding the early years.

Christina, Di, and Stacey for the decades of friendship, and sticking around for the long haul.

Anne, my surrogate mom, who always listens and who witnessed the change. Thanks for helping with my daughter, during the crucial years.

Family, and extended family, we are all connected.

Andi for your daily support, and for being by my side at the first festival, and many more. Through thick and thin, but especially for the abundant laughter (chihuahua wood).

My sister-in-law, for loving my brother and caring for my parents.

My brother, for shared memories and our love of the creek. A good and decent man, and a wonderful "bro."

My parents, for the gifts and the lessons.

My husband, for loving me like no other. Missing you still. The catalyst for this latest journey.

My step-children for sharing a bit of your lives with me. His legacy lives on.

My daughter, for the gift of being your Mom. You were my first labor of love, and the greatest emotional experience I've known. I'm so proud of the independent woman you are. Love you to the moon and back.

My higher power, spirit guides, angels, and loved ones for allowing me to *see* and *know*.

My First
Tarot Reading Event

The Healing Arts Festival

About the Author

Erin G. Burrell was born and raised in
Sacramento, California.
You can contact her through her website at
egbtarot.com
or through email at
eblucky58@gmail.com.

Made in the USA
San Bernardino, CA
21 September 2018